A Poet Drives a Truck

A Poet Drives A Truck:

Poems by and about Lowell A. Levant

Edited by
Ronald F. Levant
Carol L. Slatter
Caren E. Levant

Printed in the United States of America.

ISBN: 978-0-615864-45-7

The seven poems by Lowell Levant from *Poems Read in the Spirit of Peace & Gladness.* copyright © 1966 by Peace and Gladness Co-Op Press, are reprinted by permission of Doug Palmer/Peace and Gladness Co-Op Press.

The four poems from the Bancroft Library Archives, University of California, Berkeley ("For Doug," New Born Spiders," "Racing/Forgetting," "To the Berkeley Police Department") are from the following collections: BANC CD 376:2 and BANC CD 682:33-34, Berkeley Poetry Conference 1965 and Berkeley Poetry Conference, Young Poets from the Bay Area, The Bancroft Library, University of California, Berkeley. Reprinted by permission.

The sixteen poems by Lowell Levant and the two poems by Will Staple from *Coyote Run: Poems by Will Staple, Gene Anderson, Lowell Levant* are reprinted by permission of Gene Anderson/Anderson Publications.

The four poems by Kenneth Irby ("Waiting at the Mediterraneum for Bean and Lowell," "Strawberry Canyon Poem," "We Might Say Poetry," and "The Eye / circles, and seeks") are from *The Intent On: Collected Poems, 1962-2006* by Kenneth Irby, published by North Atlantic Books, copyright © 2009 by Kenneth Irby. Reprinted by permission of the publisher.

Front cover photo: ©Rainer Plendl/ 123RF.COM
Back cover photo: ©mg1408/123RF.COM
Section artwork: ©dervish37/123RF.COM

Table of Contents

Preface
Gene Anderson

Lowell Levant bore one of the purest and most lyrical poetic voices of the wild and wondrous 1960s in Berkeley, and continued to write and read inspired poetry until his sad passing in 2010. He perfectly captured the plain-speech style of that era, and then went on to transcend it in highly personal poetry that carefully described his world in realistic but intense, concentrated, and evocative images. Much of his finest and most mature work describes his life as a trucker and equipment driver, a lifeway that gave him time for meditation and philosophy. Other poems describe the natural world of the Bay Area and the Sierra Nevada. Like the great Chinese Buddhist poets, Lowell could make the simplest and smallest things shine with enough radiance to illuminate any darkness. His poems were carefully written, using minimal phrasing to arouse the most intense experiences in readers and hearers. This book presents Lowell's collected works, and many poems by his close friends and family—a highly talented group, and much influenced by Lowell's work. Most shared the Berkeley experience, often as fellow students of Gary Snyder. All have continued to write in the spare but vivid and luminous style that Lowell perfected.

Gene Anderson is Professor of Anthropology Emeritus, University of California, Riverside, and author of many books, including: *The Food of China*, and *The Pursuit of Ecotopia*.

Introduction
Ronald F. Levant

Lowell A. Levant (1944-2010) was born in St. Paul, MN. His father served in the Navy, in the Construction Battalion, or 'Seabees,' during WWII. After the war the family moved to South Gate, CA, where his father was a printer and his mother a homemaker. Lowell played the trombone in the South Gate school band, and graduated from Fairfax High School in Los Angeles. He initially attended U. C. L. A. but then transferred to the University of California, Berkeley. At Berkeley, Lowell was active in the Free Speech Movement in 1964, and was arrested in the Sproul Hall Plaza sit-in. After the prolonged and dispiriting trial, he withdrew from Berkeley and enrolled in the VISTA program, working with migrant workers in California's Central Valley. Upon completing the program, he became eligible for the draft, in the midst of the Vietnam War. He sought and obtained conscientious objector status, and performed alternate service in Indio, CA, where he served alongside Gary Williams. Following in the footsteps of an earlier generation of "proletarian poets" and other intellectuals who then worked as longshoremen (such as Eric Hoffer), Lowell would have the twin vocations of poet and truck driver.

Readers of Lowell's poems will notice four main qualities. First, as observed by his mentor Gary Snyder (personal communication, 6/19/12), there is "... the complex depth of his writing about work, machinery, trucks, equipment, repair, maintenance -- all in a deceptively slightly befuddled voice that masks the surprising competence of what's being actually done. These poems have a unique presence in the real world, and they have great confidence and firmness; and are free of self-pity or whining in any way (unlike so many other lesser poets of his era)." Second, there is attunement with nature, characteristic of the "Deep Ecology" poetry of Gary Snyder. Third, there is musicality, which he also created when he played a Jew's harp, sang, or strummed his guitar. Finally, Lowell's poetry often took the form of the unfiltered, unfettered, free-associative declarations of the Beat Poets of his time, particularly those of Allen Ginsberg, whom Lowell admired. However, as noted by Eileen Adams (personal communication, 5/9/12), Lowell's close friend and fellow poet: "Lowell's free associative writing was tighter and came back down to earth to make sense or a joke." Lowell's principle mentor was Gary Snyder, who was his teacher at U.C., Berkeley. While Snyder is often described as the "Poet Laureate of Deep

Ecology," he is also thought of as one of the Beats, serving as the inspiration for the main character, Japhy Ryder, in Jack Kerouac's *The Dharma Bums*. Snyder has said: "The term Beat is better used for a smaller group of writers ... the immediate group around Allen Ginsberg and Jack Kerouac, plus Gregory Corso and a few others. Many of us ... belong together in the category of the San Francisco Renaissance. ... Still, Beat can also be defined as a particular state of mind ... and I was in that mind for a while (Parini & Candlish Millier, 1993)."

Lowell enrolled in Gary Snyder's Poetry Workshop, when Snyder was a visiting faculty member at the University of California, Berkeley, during the 1964-1965 academic year. His classmates included Will Staple, Eileen Adams, Laura Dunlap, Jim Wehlage, Gene Fowler, Gail Dusenbery, and Hilary Ayers.

Lowell was first published in the *Occident*, the U. C., Berkeley, literary magazine. The title alone heralded his unique poetic presence, "To a Fog-Covered Moist Carpet of Precarious Rivers, Pussy Brambles, Eucalyptus, Moss and Cow-Dung, Just East of Tilden with a Fence around it," a title which Lowell regarded as "inspired." The poem has been well received, being republished several times.

The Berkeley Poetry Conference was held at California Hall at the University of California, Berkeley, from July 12 to 24, 1965, and provided a forum for leaders of what had then been termed a "revolution in poetry" to read their poetry and discuss their perspectives in seminars, lectures, individual readings, and group readings. The roster consisted of: Robin Blaser, Robert Creeley, Ed Dorn, Richard Duerden, Robert Duncan, Allen Ginsberg, Joanne Kyger, Ron Loewinsohn, Charles Olson, Gary Snyder, Jack Spicer, George Stanley, Lew Welch, Ken Irby, Jim Koller, David Schaff, and John Wieners. During the conference Charles Olson was designated "President of Poets," and Allen Ginsberg "Secretary of State of Poetry." Robert Creeley stated: "There will never be another poetry conference in Berkeley; Berkeley is too bizarre." (Berkeley Poetry Conference, no date).

The conference was immensely popular, and soon grew too big for the allocated space and time. People participated in any way they could. Some even perched on the ledges of open windows of California Hall to listen to the "Revolution." Lowell himself found a spot on a narrow ledge, a photograph of which is part of the UC Berkeley Archives. Denner (no date) recalls: "Paul X and I climbed up at random and found ourselves outside Robert Creeley's workshop. There were a number of these workshops going on each day for two weeks and it was warm and the windows were open, and Creeley was saying, 'There is a war; there is not a war,' and Duncan said, 'Why don't you let those guys come in,' and Creeley said, 'Sure, why not?' and we hopped in, sat ourselves down and joined the I.W.W. of Poetry." Due to the popularity of the conference, an extra day, July 25th, was added so that the growing crowds could hear from the "Young Poets from the Bay Area," who would be introduced by Gary Snyder and included Gene Fowler, Jim Wehlage, Eileen Adams, Doug Palmer, Sam Thomas, Gail Dusenbery, Drum Hadley, Lowell Levant, and Jim Thurber. Lowell read seven poems. It was at this conference that Lowell received mentoring from Allen Ginsberg. He later attributed some of his inspiration to Ginsberg, who helped him to free his mind so as to not edit his thoughts while composing poetry.

Berkeley was a bizarre place to be in the 1960s. "J. Poet" (no date) captures the spirit of that time and place in the following passage:

> What can I say about Berkeley, San Francisco and the Bay Area in the 1960s? How to convey the giddy sense of infinite possibility that hung in the air? You didn't need pot, hash, or acid to get high. There was a feeling of weightlessness permeating the air. Every day was sunny, everybody smiled, students at UC Berkeley almost danced down the street on the way to class. The air was cleaner, purer, sweeter. The streets were litter free — this is actually true. People didn't lock their doors, strangers began talking on a street corner and became life-long friends, poets and musicians were everywhere, soon to reinvent the way America produced art and made music.... Everything was possible, love was all around us, the world was changing fast and my new student and political and street friends (soon to be called hippies) were making those changes happen.

A big part of the Berkeley and S. F. poetry scene centered around the I.W.W. (The Industrial Workers of the World), which provided a home for the "Artists, Musicians, Poets, and Sympathizers Local," members of which read at the I.W.W. Hall on Minna Street in San Francisco. Doug Palmer (who, as the street poet with the *nom de plume* "Facino," wrote poems near Sather Gate at the U.C., Berkeley campus for passersby in exchange for whatever they wanted to give), edited *Poems Read in the Spirit of Peace and Gladness.* This anthology was published to showcase many of the poets who had attended the Berkeley Poetry Conference in July, 1965, and who read at the I.W.W. Hall from March-September 1965, seven months of readings, one reading each month, which were characterized as "loose" and "open." The anthology was "meant to congratulate the poets who took part, and to commemorate the spirit of those readings." It was dedicated to, among others, "Gary Snyder, whose poetry workshop class at Cal. Berkeley served as a centering point." (Palmer, 1966). Lowell's poem "Peace and Gladness" opened the volume, and Palmer borrowed its title for the title of the anthology. This poem was a later version of "I Love What I Bind to Me" (a twist on a line in a Robert Duncan poem, "I bind what I love to me"), which Lowell read at the Berkeley Poetry Conference. Lowell had eight poems in this anthology.

Another focus for Berkeley poets was COSMEP, the Conference of Small Magazine Editors and Pressman, based in Berkeley, which published *The Anthology of Poems Read at COSMEP (the Conference of Small Magazine Editors and Pressman)*, in Berkeley, California, May 23-26, 1968, and the Aldeberan Review (no date), both of which published Lowell's poems.

Lowell lived with his close friend, the poet Kenneth Irby, for many years in Sam Thomas's old house on Russell Street in Berkeley, and they mutually influenced each other. Irby read at the Berkeley Poetry Conference (although, unfortunately the recording of his reading was lost). Irby contributed four poems to the proposed volume that were written about or to Lowell. Irby (personal communication, 5/30/12 and 6/10/12) recounted how he met Lowell in the Spring of 1967: "& there is the poem, "Enkidu," Lowell read the night I first met him – a group reading somewhere on Telegraph, Robert Duncan & I went to -- & I was very struck by that poem indeed, that someone was writing a poem about that figure from Gilgamesh, not something that showed up in poetry readings in those parts in those days! & the force & power of the imagination at work (note the shift to the first person & what's involved at that point, on to the end). I asked Ruth Palmer who that was, & she told me & introduced us!"

Lowell was also very close with Will Staple, a classmate in Snyder's class, to whom he dedicated one of his poems at the Berkeley Poetry Conference. They travelled periodically to Havasupai, Arizona, and visited friends among the Havasupai tribe. During a sweat lodge ceremony, Lowell was given the name Cacoat, which means Brown Fox, and Will was named Cathot (Coyote). Lowell invoked his Havasupai name in the poem "Slipping a Shade Below." The visits to Arizona often began with a stop in Riverside, California to see another long-time friend, Gene Anderson. The collaboration between these three poets led to the publication of *Coyote Run* in 1978. Staple and Anderson each contributed poems to the present volume.

The proletarian theme of truck-driving mentioned earlier became quite important in Lowell's work, as reflected in the poems "A Poet Drives a Truck," "Transmission Linkage," "Truck Stop," "To a Teamster Comrade," "The Chain of Unemployment," and "Wheels and Gears of Beauty," and in his collection entitled "Bearing Links," which he submitted for the Henry Joseph Jackson Award in 1978.

Lowell read poetry in unforgettable way. Gene Anderson (personal communication, 5/6/12) recalled:

> *The last time I saw him, he and Will [Staple] stopped by my house about three or four years ago and we got him to read through all the poems in COYOTE RUN, including "Transmission Linkage." Lowell was always a consummate reader. He had a gentle, slow, serious voice, but he would sound playful during the surrealistic passages and musical or chant-like for the rhymed and internally-rhymed lines. He would also drift into a workingman's conversation style for the technical and mechanical riffs, as in "Transmission Linkage." His voice was always cadenced and expressive, soft but rich. He never overstated--no drama, no romantic excess--but he was never boring; he conveyed a rich, deep emotionality, never monotonous, always varying with the material. I would always get choked up--as I do now, reading the poems and hearing his voice in my mind. Farewell, guide.*

Finally, Lowell was a truly unique person, to whom other people felt deeply connected, but at the same time there was a sense that, as Doug Palmer put it, Lowell's feet seemed to not touch the ground. Lowell knew that he danced to a different drummer. His self-awareness about this and other aspects of his personality was reflected in several poems, particularly "Easily Changeable With Nevertheless Appropriate Contrasting Facets," "Why Am I So?," the untitled poem "So characteristic of me to blunder…," and the last paragraph of "Transmission Linkage." Eileen Adams (personal communication, 5/9/12) wrote: "In sum: Lowell was a humble Shaman-poet who was lonely, at times, like the rest of us, and had accomplishments and doubts, like the rest of us. In his poems he didn't seem to let it get him down for long because he could easily find the humor and fun in his everyday tasks and adventures. He slipped easily back and forth between ephemeral and "down-home" good ole boy rhythms to gift us with his delightful vision."

This volume follows the chronology just recited in regard to previously published and collected work. It begins with poems read at the Berkeley Poetry Conference, followed by work published in *Poems Read in the Spirit of Peace and Gladness*. Next comes poems read and published in various sources in the 1960s and 1970s including the *Aldeberan Review* (no date), and *The Anthology of Poems Read at COSMEP (the Conference of Small Magazine Editors and Pressman), in Berkeley, California, May 23-26*, 1968. We then turned to the later 1970s, with Lowell's collection titled "The Bearing Links" submitted for the Henry Joseph Jackson Award in 1978, and his poems published in *Coyote Run*, also in 1978. I believe that "The Bearing Links" includes what Lowell considered his best work at that point in time, as he had written to Caren Levant in 1980 that he had held back some of his best work from *Coyote Run*, because Fred Bruncke of Shaman Drum Press was planning to publish a solo volume of his work (which regrettably never occurred). Next is a selection of Lowell's unpublished work, both early and more recent, including his last poem, written in 2009, "A Visit Near Bald Peak." This section includes some longer untitled and unfinished poems which were important pieces that he had invested a lot of effort in. Finally, there is a selection of poems about Lowell, contributed by Kenneth Irby, Will Staple, Doug Palmer, Gene Anderson, and Caren Levant, his niece, who he referred to in the poem "From Tilden to Tamalpais on the Magic Carpet Ride," read at the Berkeley Poetry Conference.

References

Aldeberan Review # 3 (no date).

The Anthology of Poems Read at COSMEP (the Conference of Small Magazine Editors and Pressman), in Berkeley, California, May 23-26, 1968.

Berkeley Poetry Conference (no date). Wikipedia. http://en.wikipedia.org/wiki/Berkeley_Poetry_Conference

Denner, R (no date)   Preface to Berkeley Daze. http://www.bigbridge.org/BD-PRE.HTM

Parini, J., & Candlish Millier, B (1993) *The Columbia History of American Poetry* . New York: Columbia University Press.

Palmer, D. (1966). Editor's note, *Poems Read in the Spirit of Peace and Gladness.* Berkeley, CA: Peace and Gladness Co-op Press

Poet, J. (no date). Forward and Beyond. From Berkeley Daze. http://www.bigbridge.org/BD-FOR.HTM

Staple, W., Anderson, G, & Levant, L. (1978). *Coyote Run.* Grand Terrace, CA: Anderson Publications.

Poems Read at the Berkeley Poetry Conference

Editors' Note: Four poems read at the Berkeley Poetry Conference not included in this section were later published in <u>Poems Read in the Spirit of Peace & Gladness</u> and are included in that section: To a Fog-Covered Moist Carpet of Precarious Rivers, Pussy-Brambles, Eucalyptus, Moss, Cow Dung – Dead and Alive, Uneven and Unordered, Just East of Tilden, with A Fence Around it; A Mode of Relation (for Eileen Adams); Orange Grove (probably in Southern California); and Peace and Gladness

From Tilden to Tamalpias on the Witches' Carpet

Edges curled, the carpet rises, shakes
                    out its dust, braces, and arcs.
over fog-draped meadows facing east
                    on Contra Costa Hills,
where spider webs swell on the river-making green
and launch moon-lilies. The moon waxes
            full, turns to the Bay, lights up
            gray water pockets, and passes
            in front of luminous clouds
which attempt to keep it in their clutches.
                    without a howl
Muir Woods' wind leaves salt on my
                    niece Caren's cheek,
creeps through the loose-webbed vines
                    that pad the floor
and sifts & rearranges those vagrant
        red wood twigs that always belong somewhere
            else in this pattern.
Laurel trunks rest deaf. From their scars
branches shoot straight up to the light
and make a dense forest spacious.

Strawberry Canyon

Thick chaparral trail
spider webs cling to my face
I step firm on the fresh mud
a thin groove a bent branch
a low clump of mud spattered leaves
slip in the dark mud and nettles in the hands
gloomy bay and bunched together buildings
Contra Costa ranges draw mist from the Arroyos
rustle of ridge grass in this clearing just below chaparral knoll
deer out of hiding
slim game trail to the dirt road cut into the salt slopes
motorcycle ruts smooth out in the mud
precarious shiny slugs
baby lizard with smooth brown white skin
deer crashes into willow brush
last bird sounds of day
this incense cedar grove shades the dirt road deep green
walk faster
but watch for slugs

To a Mouse I Dreamed I Killed

I flung you up the stairs
'cause you were in my bed
I was in a strange house
and took advice from others
while carrying you in my hand

Berkeley has the same smog as LA
and freeway on-ramps, suburbs
grass dried gold
on a paved hill with a fence on top of it

I could carry you without cringing
but wouldn't take the advice
of those who had been there longest --
my brother wasn't there

turned out I thought the guy
who'd been there least long
was best to listen to
and I threw you up
like a shot put

I found you
your tail curled
your back legs collapsed, deformed
your mouth bloody
and blood on the grass

Maybe that's why people eat sprayed food
and breathe in poisoned air
conditioned for human consumption

At least I've improved
hardly wash organic lettuce
even though I've found bugs on my plate

A couple of years ago at Mammoth Lakes
down on my stomach writing letter
when lizard climbed my ass

I jumped up
and ran down road
a quarter mile
Steve can't stop telling that story
He thought it must have been a rattler
or a hungry mountain lion
though I still put moss down
with a slight jerk of chill

Maybe when I meet up with you, mouse
I'll let you go your own way

Poems from *Poems Read in the Spirit of Peace and Gladness* (1966)

PEACE AND GLADNESS

Respond to what I'm bound up with, consent
to love, so that it may be free.
                    Expect cut glass
fog in arroyos, bare rock ridges, lizards under stone,
horse flies, dung trails, sea shells,
dead mackerel and jellyfish, oil
on the water.
            Words in my mouth, sprites
at the edge of my skin and shining
            on the sill of my field.

Dark clouds over the bay
Patches of bright on the water.

We've got too much / too
            little we need do.   Forced lines
and a bunch of shed from a gopher snake
that Eileen picked up and we thought was a rattler's.
                        I followed the man
up Mission to Third –
            two quick steps and his arm burst out
with corresponding WHELP from his belly-voice—
up Market, crowds of amused, dodging them
to continue his ritual, and he
went into Woolworths to buy candy on sale.

I almost didn't pick those flowers. Smelled them:
sickly sweet domestic flowers have: furry purple balls with
gold tipped strands / on a tree
                Regent St. near Dwight Way.

Walked almost to Telegraph before turning back.
Gave them away to smilers, with
            Rhododendron and blue-red male flower
just beginning to bud.

I give you herbs:
sea whack, blessed thistle, catnip, cornsilk,
burdock root, cascara bark, buckram leaves,

acacia gum tears, chamomile flowers, couch grass, hops,
 hyssop, bay berry bark, calmas root, senna pods,
balm of gilead buds, gentian, manna.
I stood tickled in herbshop window
in downtown San Francisco.

I give you a Jay's belly, and Robins crunching at 5 a.m.
Dumb Towhees hiding behind a leaf, and Sparrows perched
                    on a fence or strutting scattered in an empty
                    parking lot.
The yawn of the man in the Impala
                    and the synchronous yawn of the man
                    in the Volkswagen, coming home
from work.
                    The barber sitting on customer chair
at back of sixteen barber mirror shop
closed up for the night, smoking
a cigarette. The arab
                    following with his eyes the blond lady
in white short tennis dress
that he nearly ran down on his bike.
The boy / jerking his head to put on his coat
coming off the bus.
                    Facino's face lit up as he makes a poem:
his forehead lifting, his eyes opening wide
smiling with his mouth closed,
                              or when he
covers lips to keep straight face
as Jeff Poland races and slides on his shoe soles
to answer phone during reading.
Union Square pigeons blessing Gene Fowler's Shaman Songs,
                                        flying
all together from the statue, the sun behind them,
shitting on Gene's head.
                    Tad playing with Ruth
dragging her ragged, both of them puffing and open mouthed
                                        smiling.
Eileen crouched in the marsh putting Tiger Frogs to sleep
caressing the neck, distrustful of her power.
Astri standing on her bed, her arms stretched out and circling
to make a point. And Tove like a little girl

jumping up from her seat to indicate assent.
I give you my stumbles and lumps in the throat.
<u>What</u> <u>is</u> is what you expect, and expect the best, for

Old men will die and leave their curse;
Young men too eager to fight
will spoil their elders' chances
to prove themselves what they are not.
Irreversible past and webbed up present
                    so that when you cut your bonds
You leave the trace of your attempt.

*Editors' Note: An earlier version of this poem was read at the Berkeley Poetry
Conference, and was titled "I Love What I Bind to Me." The title was a twist on a
line in a Robert Duncan poem, "I bind what I love to me."*

For a Woodsey Friend

i'm just sitting round here saying horseshit and belching
after 5, gray dawn, 10 minutes bird noise
                    remembered your birthday
should be soon or late   so wrote the above garbage
how can i get enthused over april grass on dwight way foot-
                                          hills
                resisting and submitting to the wind
the rain the day before had freed from the golden gate
scumming the bay view we watched from that hillside
blowing your hair all over your head as we walked to
a peaceful grove of sugar pine   your lithe legs folding
                on that needle bed floor
and talking about important things
                revolutions and all
your waist that i hold every now and again on a tree branch
or what seems like a tree branch
Blue Red/spots on my cigarette   damn capitalists
                uh/what I want to say
is/ i think you deserve all kinds of nice things said on your
        birthday so why dont you just think of all the nicest things
        you want said and think that i said them
oh that won't work because you'll think of the wrong nice things
or if your mood is subject to the same alterations or alternations
        —changes—as my mood is subject to   you'll think
of un-nice things and attribute them to me… why don't you
just convince yourself im saying all kinds of nice things to you
        and then start/   .   try to think of
nice things and forget the un-nice things you think and think
        i thought and/or am thinking what's left.

ORANGE GROVE (probably in Southern California)

I wake up lying on dry leaves and oranges
                        covered head to thigh
hard sponge pile of steady dropping fruit.
Crushed leaves dissolve in hot water
                        sprout petunias and lilacs
decay the stems and launch them into the sky.
The oranges roll into my clothes, till I look like
                        a blimp or a fat cheap cigar
exploding and fragmenting my underwear into dust.
I tumble down this river, speed
                        ahead of the flow, till at the ocean
splat on the concrete river bank. A band of howling drunk
                                                women
                        out on a Bacchanal or on the way to play Bridge
pick me up and carry me into their temple – a shack
                        with boarded up windows.
A fairy with her short skirt flaring out
                                dances incessantly round
                                a statue of a gigantic cock
                                or mushroom.
They put me on a table blow me many times limp
                                run their teeth
                                up and down
                                & spit out blood.
I grab thighs from evry where and taste orange juice.

Editors' Note. This poem, when read at the Berkeley Poetry Conference, was "dedicated to Bill Staple."

A Mode of Relation
(for Eileen Adams)

Boulder at southeast end of Stinson Beach
Junction Panoramic Drive, Highway 1, Dipsea Trail
Looking out on Pacific Ocean, Bolinas Lagoon, Point Reyes
Summer foothills, high gold grass
Backing and trusting with a dry whirr
Thistle-click in the strong wind
Seaside Paintbrush, Locoweed, Vetch,
Wide opened Red Maids,
Blue-Eyed Grass, Tidy Tips,
Poppies, and Sunflowers.
Barnswallows watering in pond
             just up Dipsea Trail
Baby Tiger Frogs in the moist marsh grass
We talked about what sort of children we had been, and danced
back down the trail
           with beer warmed loins, picking
the wildflowers, the rustic male ones too, and the furry grass
           by the pond. It was all
sycamore
then, because that sounds nice.

Adon Olom

Big dog tied to a tall fat tree
The leash
best
because he's big
The leash
short
because it's been
wound once round the tall fat tree
Small dog runs, dodges, misses
the honorable, angry big dog.
Adon Olom Asher Moloch
Asher Ruehē_Ding Ding Sollee
Little dog sharpens chin on wet grass
pants, waits
for breath to come back.
Fast feet bounce on cold wet grass
rush on leaves
disturb the sleep.
Little dog darts a few more times
Big dog unwinds once round the tree.
The leash
long
The breath
short and little dog
catches feet on leash.
Big dog looks
Regrets long leash.
Small dog free
then big dog caught
The tree stoops over
sprouts long white beard
wears a skullcap and a frilly shawl.
The tree bends back
and begins to sing:
Adon Olom Asher Moloch
Diddly Bom Zu Da Waih.
Big dog gets free
bends to sex
finds they're the same
smiles ashamed.
The band starts playing
Small dog bounces off.

THE HARVEST

Wrap the rough string around the vines
                    until the dew dries off,
wind the twine around the sticks and look around –
                    (Ginny and Carol
                        (moving ahead talking with the rest of the crew
                            (hands blistered and stinging –
                                        (bug poison)
tie it off at the end of the row.

HOLD THINGS FULL

Ever notice those burly men
who squeeze your shoulders
and can't talk
            without standing up square
who have their whole weight behind them
                    as they
                follow your moods
with their eyes, and snap back
                    straight & centered, from taut gut strings
                    and an even follow through. hmmm
mmm hmmm?
step slow but firm
on the loose rock
                    of the steep hillside.
        Pick up a rock
grasp it full
                        hold it up to the moon.
                    Cover yourself with fertile black soil
fertilize it with your own shit
            and sleep there.
        Yell back
to the coyotes. Move along with all
                        the critters:
rocks & tide   jays   trees

Poems Read and Published in Various Sources in the 1960s and Early 1970s

Gliding Quilt

Take a wish with you
        leaving gold behind
    up the cavern waves away
                guilt sticks in the throat
gone out a flutter
            the same impulse that confirms memory
                smoke in rainbows, the
conversion gently slaked, rust remains
before the whirlpool drums let out
            flame tucks into wind
        could be glad to rest upon
        a side of dreamless flesh
        where over rains must call

    the gentle voice of Aaron is our
best chance, he'd be pleased to
                though he don't know any better
            than we do what's going on

-believe that's fair, shouldn't wait till
            anyone finds out, you can
            even use my tambourine
except to bail out water

17 August 1967

Editors' note: From The Anthology of Poems Read at COSMEP, the conference of Small-Magazine Editors & Pressman, in Berkeley, California, May 23-26, 1968. *Edited by Richard Krech and John Oliver Simon, an Undermine Press — Aldeberan Review Book*

2 20 68

Memory, how far wide takes me
snatching that I grasp
               drat fidget goddam
the cypress roots that clamp onto cliffs
having a source in the impenetrable
                    depths of eternity – this like
an old voice that weaves in
collaging fragments of sound
          not usually making any sense
challenging with ornery arbitrariness
               of gesture, where the dance rhythm
               proceeds from the foot falls
a grave voice – wet and dark with resonance
                    careful now the splinters
                    and shatter patterns
                    clumps of reeds at river mouth
                    that you can take any one
                    so long as it rains – African Queen
Bogart kicking his engine
steam valve clogged with screwdriver
that he could remove but likes having a machine that he has to kick
to make it work

ii

Tulip in the watershed
Magnolia drifting downstream
how does a fly choose direction?
does a hawk ever get lost?
After I've been walking in the mud awhile
I like to sit down and peel it off my boots

iii

There are four reasons
but I can't remember which comes first
four memories that proceed one from the other, that I might just
have not even mentioned
has that ever happened to you?

where you get stoned looking back and back around
          fly-buzzed, bristling with perplexity
I shall go out into the day
uncross my legs and pluck the cobwebs from off my eyes
or just let the wind mat them into a birthplace
an organic pillow – a sentimental waking into pulse and flesh
It was good I could count them
                    if that wasn't just arbitrary either
I've crossed my legs again
it wasn't four, that was just a number
for someone else's convenience
that drat fidget good goddam
only developed after "the flowing river of incalculable moments
of consciousness having its source in the impenetrable depths of
eternity"
                    moved a smooth stone
               from its bed to start an island
kicking up dirt and silt
                    fresh wind entering
               through the balcony
          no wiser than a beard
                    less white with shorter strands
               braided beards
                    rollicking quilt patches
          strands of hair
          bobbing in the wind
          before my eyes
there are three wool clothed hikers high-stepping round a bend
swinging their arms in song for swish

                                   iv

The point of my pen shadow
the shadow of my hand
                    overwhelming like phlegm
   fleggum my fledgling
          flogging in bowl weevil country
oh what am i flogging except that it sloshes
          dear Lisa my weav'ly wife
evil weasel   pen prick   lark spur
lake in pine shadow   gophers, buzzards, beavers

fenugreek, cardamom, tarragon
tarry long Talleyrand / which direction gliding buzzard?
burrowing gopher   hibernating by night
where the reeds are thick with leeches
and the air is heavy with Bogart in Africa
magnolia drifting downstream
the wool clothed hikers singing
          comically their song wrapped in balloon
          pulsating as the light plays on the fog their breath makes
                    in the cold
makes my feet quiver
and my head strong
strung with springing
coffee and tobacco
noise in the coffee houses: music on radio, people talking
clatter of dishes, whistling
               last week in full moon
          I sat on a hillslope of Eucalyptus
          that the road interrupting
made me think they were separate / all of this here I hear I hear
the noise of the cars roaring that full moon, cold
and I thought I wanted ice cream
all together, indistinct i fart
and there is no choice, no power beyond the melody
collaged from these   occasions
nothing is lost
time only loses
               in a lifetime
     what another time gains
that I came here for the roar
and the fist swinging clatter
of violins – violence
     vile but living
     that I try to deny
       or qualify to consent
like narrowing air through tubes
hearing the roar of growth
swift as the wag of a dog's tail.

*Editors' note: From Aldeberan Review #3, no date. A different version of this poem
was published as "Sitting Upstairs with the Windows Wide Open," in Coyote Run.*

The Redeeming Power in Storms and Steep Cliffs

Wilderness insight gets
Developed like a post hole dug out, or
Star drill carved shaft in a granite wall
From hammering in an iron stake 4 x 10

Then you can learn how to do without
whatever you give up in the way of civilized comfort
only there's a gap between
when you give up and when you do without
for the seed to develop
It's got to be set in there deep

                    —so says Shorty as he takes a drink
                          and passes it to me
                 like night vision, I say

And food too, if you're hungry enough
that plant will signal you to eat of it

Best acorns a mile and a half upstream
Wild oats to thresh at the right time
Stay with you all day
In a barrel or oil drum   rolled around
                       till the chaff fluffs off
Blow it out with a bellows   (or the pot-shaped breathing
Huge fingers and gears mesh to thresh and polish
Houses can be torn down in a day
Staked posts are good to lean on when the winds rage.

2-72

Editors' note: Read at "Open Reading #2, Fall 1972, David Bromige, California State University Sonoma."

For Doug

The band playing such corny music
& so many people walking
                    round bug-eyed
That man with his daughter on
                    his
          shoulders, ride him
horsy—crazy—corn & sugar candy
it would seem
This is a Saturday afternoon
               small town
band concert —

New-born Spiders

Canopies flying —

Setting sails unset for other fields, another ground —

Canopies flying —

Making a risk of the wind / to settle them in the grass.

Racing   /   Forgetting

Stevie Schwarz is running around like the universe
will collapse and fold us inside out of it
tomorrow or the next breath
                racing to make sure things will go smoothly
                        so that this bit of time will be all right
"We all suspect that will happen to us but we forget it."
                        "Forget it," said the man
            to the cop beginning to harass him, the man investigating
an arrest   "Forget it," the ex-southern california freddie
                ex-psych major now mustachioed hipster said when
                        he failed to
            make his point
we all say when we don't care to finish what we've started
                        say but don't believe
            the thot of leaving something unfinished gnawing at us
the wires of the mobile we don't know how to balance
                        curling up and tangling in a mess
gnawing at the businessman racing home in his super-padded
Oldsmobile
                        his briefcase on the seat full of unfinished work
                            nor ready to fit just right
                            this night either
the teeth of gears we thot fit   gnaw at our purpose
and springs we've placed, poised to them snap into the spokes
our determination tensed into the spokes, depending
                        on the center of the wheel, where there is nothing.

November 1966

To The Berkeley Police Department

Thank you for your big father arms –
And thank you for your lovingkindness wisdom – O hawk eyes,
O dance the people,
            Around the fire pit with bundles of medicine bay

The Bearing Links:
Collection Submitted for the Joseph Henry Jackson Award (1978)

Easily Changeable With Nevertheless Appropriate Contrasting Facets

At the Tiger's Run in Hangchow, sometimes stayed
    the mad monk, Laid-lo.
He never meditated, fasted, or prayed to excess.
He hung around cheap places of public entertainment
    dispensing charms and advice
      to the poor folks out having a good time.
Birds flocked to him. Children followed him around.
Wild animals approached unafraid.
Flowers turned their heads towards him.

Occasionally some junkyard or corner of the universe
    inspired him to great seriousness.
He would swing from one smattering of specialized knowledge
    to another branch, regardless of context.
With certain discriminating companions
    easily bent to each other's whims of the moment
    he thrived on intricacies.

Enamored of process, he never wanted to see anything end
    before he considered all the connections.
Only in the flimsiest manner would Laid-lo bring his account
    back to the origins, before he became engrossed
    once again in the manner of his report.
    He was capable of simple and direct talk
    in the dialect of the area
    whether he was speaking with tea-carriers from Szechuan
    or Lolo bandits of the rugged mountain passes.

He also wrote aesthetic treatises of great complexity.
He energetically participated in the common work
    and did not consider what was his share
    or whether the task be menial.
From people engaged in projects beyond his comprehension
    he absorbed very little useful information
    but much about their personal styles
    remained with him.
People who were primarily interested

in the what and the how
knew better than to allow him
to indulge in leisurely association.
The specific facts were not entirely irrecoverable
but interspersed with elaborate discoveries
in which he cast widely diverse spells.

His eyes would gleam as he let his mind dwell
in its opaque labyrinth
of increasingly involuted digressions.

Editors' Note: "Laid-lo" and "Lolo" are probably plays on Lowell's name, as he often used the nickname "Lalo."

Rig-Pa-Med-Pa

Firmly seated on my throne
(a flat space on a boulder
deep within a canyon)
I lean back against the stiff dry wind.

No words can convey how my eyes
sparkle with a searchlight glow.

When the wind subsides, the steep iron limp walls,
agave, and encelia reach out
and prop me up in the slack left behind,
never having been fettered with explanations.

Outside of my kingdom of simplicity
powerful people get out in front of me.
They tell me my place and what I'm supposed to see.
They don't care to have me act
like a Central Asian Monarch,
Astride a boulder
with the stiff wind at my back.

Nettle Sting Makes My Skin Tingle

Monkish in thirst for labyrinths, terraced caves,
catacombs of long remembered rhythms,
I carry some heavy loads
that release in the pulsing strain of sinew
a breath that traces the moonshine trail
cut to the widely circling current of power.

Off the trail in the steep, brushy canyon,
I do the dance of moving under scrub,
roll into stance, tuck into the swell,
burrow through shale, tilt my head back in the rain,
and lounge on thickly carpeted cloud forests.

Dogs lie fragrantly on plush cushioned meadows.
The sun streams in arches across the misty gulches.

Sudden sea-slap against the flat-backed rock
wears into it the soft froth of gentle restlessness.

A ferment of kinships forming and dissolving.
The yeast in the crock settles in my old notebooks.

The Spoken Wheel

In my zeal to enjoy the buds of my mind
I slap them into a sputtering skillet.
The fragrance quickly scatters all around.
Scent changes to sound as I imagine the resonance
of limestone caves behind Mooney Falls
that echo the roar over the ages,
fashioning in their organpipe chambers
a sound that only seems to be a chord.

"It reminds me of something I've never experienced."

In bodily and mental ease I search for the pinwheel center
that starts making me curious, so that I can abandon myself
to discovering the spontaneous shifts of interest
I might possibly follow.
                    Free of any humiliating losses,
Sometimes I'm a sage but mostly I'm a fool
parading across a rickety bridge.
I can swallow most misfortune, but what I inflict sticks
in my craw, pulling me down through vine tunnels
from the neck back.

No need survive
only navigate
with every turn the wheel takes.
You're the master of your fate
Only if you don't have
that much at stake.

-2-

People can't hear me unless I throw my voice out
throw it out, get rid of it, raise it above the swampy din
to navigate the wider bands
to take my stance out of my shoes
to causes above my spectrum.
So goes the injunction I misheard when I was grouchy
about overcooked broccoli and fried a pepper in a hot skillet.

Manipulative in my tentativity
rude in my polite manners
Unfair in not seeming to be selfish
I would be less of a burden on others
if I didn't try so hard to help.

To take no less than is offered
and to be generous when it is my turn to give

to avoid having to say I'm sorry
after I've gone and done what I had to do

If I had a nobler sentiment
I'd have done the same or even worse
and gotten away with it.

-3-

A slosh buckler, lord of mud and fog
with pebbles in my sandals I amble
through Bear Valley meadows, ladybug on my arm
sand in my hair, loaded with pollen
to present to my queen
who gives me no favor nor fame
but sends me out into the cold and dark
to gather more pollen
to slip under her lace.

O Dakini
I felt you beside me
knees at my back
so soft
yet we both trembled.

When I'm submerged in you
your waves rock me up
on my knees, a buoyancy there
almost standing up.
Your voice is the rushing of the creek rapids in the shallows.

I've learned to trust the downstream flow
roller-coasting feet first by the rocks
For the swiftness is equally bubbly
cushioning my descent.
In you I float
wherever the water falls.

Three Sandstone Characters On a Cliff

The wrinkles in squirrel's face
        radiate in the prayerwheel suns
        around his squinting eyes.
He is preparing a piece of his mind:

      "The trees rise to the top of the woods
       mingling their branches in patterns
       that I dangle and swing thru.
       My fluffy tail floats like a sail
       whilst I scamper dapperly
       clicking my static driven heels.
       Springs of fur sparkle on my tail
       in the branch-filtered sun-beams.
       The wind swirls in chills
       and drafts around my nose."

Standing Alligator flicks a very long, by then very cooked ash
        off his cigar, and wags his long jaws slowly:
       "Stag lives out at Stag-Nation
       which is even swampier than where I live
       covered with cobwebs and dust.
       Window pane broke one stormy night
       and muddied all the books.
       Seeds blew in and sprouted in the binding.

      "Stag's horns whistle when he runs
       and bellow in the shine from full meadow sun
       with Perky Sue and Spunky Priscilla
       growing amidst the lupine and clover.

      "He likes to trap a phrase
       change direction on a pun, and
       stealthily return to a serious
       dismissal of blame and error."

"That's because flaming arrows
        make haystacks explode.

"Eros continues in other stacks
    where little needling
    but much fondling takes place."

"Hey Stag, I'm glad to see you made it over.
We can have a toke and drink some
cranberry quicksilver beetle juice."

Hush Wind

In the lower branches of an old juniper
smooth of bark, brittle at the edges,

I wonder if I'm truly protecting myself from the wind,
for it rushes more swiftly through narrow channels,
blowing out my match as I stare up at islands of bark with lichen
and patterns of green branches with purple berries.

The bark hangs on in isolated stands. The twigs and leaves
bob in the wind and shade me from the sun.

I sit in the tree and feel the wind.
I find the matches that I truly lost before.
After a toke, I install the beer can in a cubbyhole,
so it won't spill. As the wind picks up
and a yellowjacket moves around my short branch,
I see cloud shadows across the Amadee-Skedaddles and
think of giving this natural occurrence my blessing
when the wind suddenly hushes.

In that coincidence I feel
that I'm on the right track finally.
The wind briskly wakes me back
to the pen in my hand and the rest of the beer in the can.
I missed exploiting the hush in the wind for a toke.
Hoping for another hush in the wind, I'm reluctant to move.

Holy Reverential Sidekicks

Holy reverential sidekicks, with faces to the creek bank
praise the dancing branches,
the glitter of water and leaves.

The quartz and granite bank reflects the flicker of light
and projects a shadow whiteness on the water.

This motion courses across our still gazes.
Screens of skin, sense, and breath
we heap up what
rock and water only give right back.

Generating Clouds of Enthusiasm

When you shook that mooch off
in the bar, by grabbing his collar
was that merely a friendly gesture
or did you mean a bit of intimidation?

Sly Dog said, "It was for his own good."

*Editors' note: This poem was previously read at Open Reading #2, Fall 1972,
David Bromige: California State University, Sonoma.*

The Escape

A 15¢ beer with yet ⅓ of a glass
Suddenly a pool cue tip brushed my cheek.

As I was making a u-turn, the guilty fellow
ran out, obviously to apologize.

To A Teamster Comrade

Your wariness keeps you awake
on marathon moonlight pilgrimages from Modesto to Ukiah
with a flatbed load of fruit crates cabled on.

Perhaps you would not notice the flimsy ephemera I seek
in wisps of fog, shadow patterns, and the hissing of steam
off of the hot rocks in the sweat lodge, which seem to answer
the incantations and drumming of the shaman's trance.

The old Indian doctors cannot cure any of the modern illnesses,
but they know where the good springs and traditional doctoring
places are, far away from the highway.

The spirits they cultivate will not stand for any abuse.
They have been around those sacred groves and outcrops of rock
much too long. They have more to do
than to arouse a dormant skeptic.

If I told you about the creatures of my imagination,
they would not even back me up.
They retreat into the darkness at the bark of a watchdog.

Such Shamanistic Vocables

Utterable in séance trance, certain spells
charge my voice with resonant intensity.
I, the stump-top doctor, salvage sacred sites:
cramped in a rock crevice, perched on a branch,
in the midst of manzanita, where gold was dug,
grasslands overgrazed, the rich topsoil eroded
down to the fish in the ocean, and in clear-cut places
where all the diverse plants start growing
right on top of heaps of slash.
I appeal to geomorphic deities, who dwell in creek ripples:
the texture of rock, bark, and sweat; wind-tossed leaves;
dense, varied clumps of woven grasses: echoes, thunder, stillness,
gusts of wind, coyotes, and the rapids of the creek below
sounding in the warm drafts along occasional water channels.

0 spirit of this site, come hither and hover above;
remember all the doctors who wanted to understand!
Remember their songs. These kind folk spoke with penetrating conviction
to the woods and rocks, as if they cared or had anything to do
with the people's lives.
Indeed the earth can transmit an impulse that I don't distort at all.
I search for images in the moonlit branches, but see only branches.
The log trucks and airplanes have also left behind
a physical reverberation. May those sounds fade!
If I hadn't been exploring off rock ledges, up in pine trees,
crouching thru brush, jumping from one rotting log to another,
I wouldn't be out here singing at night in this place
untrodden by cattle, a soft fragrant meadow
where my legs are at rest.

Silver Moccasin

"I never go to town anymore. If there's anything I want to buy,
I have it mailed to Rim-top and pack it down on my horse. Anytime
I go to town I get drunk and spend all my money."
Astride his horse, his hands full of Monkey Ward boxes,
Ed pointed out the ancestral trail to see Wipaha and Wipahti:
     -water carved pinnacles on the red rock shelf.
     "Put some wind in your voice: Wipaha, Wipahti.
Past the cottonwood there's a ladder, I think."

I hiked on ledges and squeezed thru rifts of rock.
No ladder   I fumbled along on narrow shelves
groping my way to the next fissure.
Bulges on the sandstone bent me backwards
as I slid sideways facing the crumbling wall
and hoped for enough space on the next shelf.

I carried a jagged piece of mirror
that I found in a dump
for a signal in case I got stuck.

After I got up there, I should have come right back down,
because it was getting dark.
Instead I made for the easier but longer Apache trail.
I followed a barranca, sliding down slick sandstone in places.
To my astonishment, it ended up on a cliff right above the village.
With 150 feet of rope I could have made it down.
The lights came on and the dogs started barking.
The rocks stayed warm till the wind came up.
I almost thought I heard angry voices couched in the wind.
Someone said he got caught up there once when he was fourteen.
     "I was grateful to be back alive."
He must have been playing me for a punk.
Wipaha was not the least bit angry, only pronouncing his name.

I gave up feeling like an alien, but rather a Mongol Monarch,
seated on a boulder with the stiff wind at my back.
Morning came sooner than I expected. I had a clear path back.

The basket weaver lady saw me drinking soda pop near the store
just after I got down. She told me next time I go up to see Wipaha
I should leave behind something shiny that I value.
A couple years later she hired me to chop down
some inaccessible creekside cottonwoods.
She had me into her house for lunch
and gave me a dollar besides.
That same year I found the ladder:
of cottonwood, willow brush, and rope.
It was so dilapidated I climbed around it.

***

Wipaha this belongs to you.
I don't want to give it up.
It looks very good on my ear.
Maybe you'd like this splicing knife instead.
It's more useful than one tiny moccasin.

Poems from *Coyote Run: Poems by Will Staple, Gene Anderson, Lowell Levant* (1978)

Juniper Scrub Mountain Shade

Across outcrops of rocks I spotted a herd of <u>Jabalis</u>:
        the wild boars in Southern Arizona that talked to Nanao.
Thru tangled brush near the top I stooped and crawled around the
trunks.

By a separate route Will spotted an unopened parachute
            that some packrats had chewed on
            exposing several layers of silk.
After we forgot it at the Ashram, Susan brought it back to Tucson,
            so that we could take it to the sierras with us
            to hang all summer on a madrone
            in the clearing where we brewed beer

At the top of the mountain we got underneath a slant boulder
in a space hollowed out with room enough to sit
            scrape a pipe of resins
            enjoy the oranges we'd saved thru such a thirst
and watch the shadows of clouds across miles of desert
            beyond lower ranges.

We got the idea of bringing students up such a mountain as this
to appoint them meditational chambers in rock caves and overhangs.
We would ask them for their grass and wine and go off with it
to a choice cave where we'd smoke and drink with a couple of women in
the class

When we returned to our students we'd be incredulous if they hadn't
achieved enlightenment. Didn't we provide everything they needed?

                    Down the mountain on the slick rock
                    of a watercourse we jumped from foothold
                    to foothold and encountered a rattler.

Slipping Out of the Morning Shade

The last of May by the swift deep Yuba
A bottle of home brew 3 months old
wedged in a crack on an underwater granite shelf

I sat on a flat rock in the morning shade
and thought about great men in remote places
who might just have minded their own business
and whose legend survives only in the local traditions
when occasional visitors had the good fortune to be around them
when they felt like telling a good one and brought out the chilled home
brew.

I lost my shade along the Tarim with an ancient sage from Turfan
and drowsily crawled back under the tree
where the rocks weren't quite as flat.

There was a way to twist to avoid all the sharp edges
and I found the flat surfaces in much the same way
as I would find footholds climbing down a rock wall
that I can't quite see the best not look at too long
but just hang there and slowly drop a foot a little further down
    till I reach a flat place
and let the rest of the limbs drop one by one.

Editors' note: This poem was previously read at the Open Mike Poetry Readings at the Starry Plough Irish Pub, 3101 Shattuck Avenue, Berkeley, CA, and previously published in "A Poemphlet from Crosscut Saw."

Stump-Top Doctoring

I found a new page as I would have founded a colony
after stumbling through the forest.
A brook and meadow with terraced slopes.
All the immortals converge from various directions
to found a colony for the space of times I sing on the stump.

Mosquito hour comes around, and I don't really want
to go anywhere because it's all so fine right here.
I just pick up a log and drag it downhill
to burn in a slash pile with the snow on the ground.

The trees bounce my song back.
Luxuriating in the feeling I imagine
in the sight of the branches at the edge of the meadow.
I negotiate the labyrinthine complexities from close at hand.

The sun has gone down on the swimming hole.
I lay upon a rock that's still warm.
In the roar of the rippling rapids
I hear the old men's sweat lodge song.

The Chain of Unemployment

I swung a chain around
till it whistled by my ears.
It once held a pen to a desk
at the unemployment office with any eye screw
that I unscrewed after closing time.

It broke off while I spun it
and flew into a puddle. I dug for it in the mud
but didn't really want it.
When the puddle dries some kid will find it.

Mary's Flat

The look downstream to the jagged cliffs:
Digger and ponderosa faintly overshadow
the steep cut cliff with etched out cathedrals
and a dotted fringe on the plateau.

A mass of cool clouds move northwest.
Lichen crops out on boulders
and the pebble slide pile
of flat, brick-size rocks.

Mining caved in the canyon walls,
so that liveoak grows aslant on the opposite bank.

China Mary built that old cabin
and cleaned houses down the canyon.
She died burning trash that had blasting caps in it.
Refugee stage-drivers moved in years later,
and built irrigation systems for a garden
using the old flumes and pipes. Upon the
mossed and lichened outcrops, the sweat-singers
built a lodge for hot rocks. Tearing down hog pens
whole walls at a time, the clan put up well-ventilated
dwellings. An old mine-shaft became a coyote den,

lantern warmed, that conducted sound from the core of the earth,
when the dormant <u>Nagas</u> were appealed to
with adequate intensity.
Slash and manzanita burned over numerous campfires,
until the barbarians broke into our cars,
smashed windows and honey jars, left almonds strewn on the road,
gunnysacks-full wasted, rather than used.

When my car was trashed I lost much of value,
but I missed most the well broken-in boots, once resoled.
The trail down the hill was a rough   one
in the dark with a pack. Boot soles wore thin.
Sharp edges became dull. In the pulsing strain
of sinew, moving up the hill, a breath escaped.
Everything that I thought I had or was
left with that breath. Answering a yodel a mile away,
I wished that I had lost more.
Bean and I carried down the roadside-killed fawn,
so that the meat would not be wasted.
When the sun hit the camp, we contested with yellowjackets
for the choice hindquarters and backstrap, fried
in commodity butter over a slash fire.
We kept it in a cave with water dripping over the entrance
until it turned blue. That was also where we chilled home brew.
Climbing up in an almond tree with a tarp down on the ground,
I filled my gunny sacks again after knocking the branches
with a rubber tire strip riveted to a baseball bat.
Though we lost more than we thought we could afford,
living on the edge taught us how to use
what was already there.

Painted Canyon Smoke Trees

The smoke trees in painted canyon wash
were mostly shriveled half brown.
A few had purple flowers
where the canyon widened out.
Desert willow with white hanging bells,
paloverde and mesquite also occupied the wash.

Truck-Stop

The grease and grit sticks
to my pores. The swirls in my hand
I decipher this morning.
The cuts heal slowly. How much I relished
the few minutes I could stand by the electric heater
gulping coffee at 4 a.m.
I didn't even have time to finish Prince Valiant.

The bolt was frozen, holding the spare tire
beneath the truck.
Out in the cold, dark mud-puddle after dawn
I took it off with an impact wrench
only after we moved the truck close enough to the air hose.
I could hardly disconnect the frisky gun.

My boss who was referred to as "a fart in a whirlwind"
found a place near his house, where I could move.
I thought he was doing me a favor
until he started coming by at all hours
asking me to fill in for someone who didn't show up.

One morning after a long night, a semi pulled up to the gas pumps.
I said "You don't want gas in that thing do you?"
The driver said "Fill that up with gas, like I said."
After I filled his diesel tanks with gas, I noticed the
five gallon gas can which he had set down in front of his cab.

The mixture of diesel and gas drained out on the concrete.
A hose washed it out to the street, where a subdivision
has since gone up. Slipping on the mixture, pushing around
a squeegee, I watched the patterns change color in the dawn.

To a Fog-Covered Moist Carpet of Precarious Rivers, Pussy-Brambles, Eucalyptus, Moss and Cow-Dung — Dead and Alive, Uneven and Unordered, Just East of Tilden, With a Fence Around It.

You move in the gazes that turn intent
        from the side, toward me,
in the smile that pulls in smoke
                and in the deliberate long puffs,
in the delicate exact turn of the breasts
                with the hand to the chin
                and to the back of the car seat
        that served as a couch,
with the forearms to the calves,
in the blinks, the finger tips, the strolls,
                and the statue of liberty pose to the West,
in the urge and in the way
to soar within the flesh —
                that ride on the witches carpet:
ambiguous and sneaky
complicated and useless
requiring order but demanding that it not be form,
for even the best shoes wear out,
while bare foot prints on the shifting sands last forever —

Finally you move in the unpracticed purrs
in my tense, tired lap, so that I may realize
you alone.

Editors' note: This poem is a later version of a poem that has been read and published several times. It was Lowell A. Levant's first published poem, in Occident, Spring 1965, edited by Laura Dunlap, Eileen Adams, and Tove Neville, Published by Associated Students of the University of California, Berkeley. Other early versions were read at the Berkeley Poetry Conference and Published in Poems Read in the Spirit of Peace & Gladness.

Hung Over in the Crotch of a Tree: Salmon Hole

How awkwardly I climbed
> a tall cottonwood overhanging the creek
> with wobbly broken steps nailed on.

Past the tenuous steps
a rope hangs from a chain hitched to a high branch
too far up for me to go that day
hung up where the steps ended
in the crotch of a tree to catch my breath.
> If people weren't watching me and yelling catcalls
> I might have stayed crotch to crotch with the tree
> till my legs stopped trembling.

I was trying to impress a lady in a group with other men.
Thinking that I would be first, I was the only one to go into the water
for a pujah: immediately out the first dip ritual.
Before that I bounded over the rocks and contemplated climbing over
all the way down the cliffs in the crevices without a rope.
My spirit was low. I puffed when I bounded and yielded to suggestion.
Instead of staying in that safe branch
I went down that wobbly ladder backwards:
> the worst way to go
> a few more feet to climb up to the next branch
> without the dubious benefit of those shamefully uncertain steps
> might even have been easier than going down that ladder

¾'s of the way down my knees sagged.
I wrapped my legs around the tree and could hardly make it the rest
of the way down to the water's edge.

Plush Wind Nectars

Holding my head high
swaggering and reeling
I tromp about on soft, damp, hilltop ground.

The breeze whips my hair; sweat trickles down.
I beat my goose-pimpled chest,
growl out boldly, and palms up
take possession of the land and wind;
my loyal subjects in an Altaic court.

I urge all you folks to make yourselves at home,
to sleep tight, not to get mosquito bite,
to piss frequently, and to show a little irritation
when you get bee-stung or fall
into nettle swamps off the trail.

Nettle sting makes my skin tingle.
Only when I get lost do I dance,
tuck into the swell, roll into stance,
and burrow through shale.

I tilt my head back in the rain
and lounge on tickly carpeted cloud forests.
Dogs lie fragrantly on plush cushioned meadows.
The sun streams in arches across the misty gulches.

I cross bridges of long remembered rhythms.
A current of power circles a ferment of kinships.
The yeast in the crock settles in my old notebooks.
With graceful awkwardness I give you my stumbles
and lumps in the throat. What is is what you expect.

Expect the best; do what you do.
Be liberal in declarations and liberal with omens.
Look forward to the ordinary with as much zeal
as to the unexpected; look forward to chance
with as much trust as to the usual.

Old men will die and leave their curse.

Young men too eager to fight
will spoil their elder's chances
to prove themselves what they are not.
Irreversible past and webbed up present.
When you cut your bounds
you leave the trace of your attempt.

Grouse Ridge Idyll

My lot to dawdle idly has been brought to crisis.
Usually there's something to find inside
when I get lost. I caught a glimmer of that
as I unnecessarily got myself immersed
in scratchy manzanita that just went on and on
up and over on the other side.
Alone I could only wander, climb a high branch
to look around, and catch spells as I lingered.
Loose shuffle of limbs,
tipped-back head, slouch pose.
Shamefacedly I struggle back the endless stretch
I'd already covered. Yet I was proud to realize
I could make that much headway were I a fugitive.

Butte Creek

Come, let me bury my head
in your shady canyon
Water trickles into a cool stream
Buttes stand tall in the sun
rocks washed of silt
branches, bark, and twigs
        within reach
            to make and stir fire
red silt washed off rocks
        plowed up downstream clumped with dead grass roots
Cottonwood seeds fill the sun-glint sky
        take hold in the pussy mucosia   make sneezes
Flowers float in water and sky
                            touchpoints thru dust film
                  Buddha's eyes, cock tips, nose hair
                    shadows of rivulets
                    folding crotchlets weaving
            through the dance of waves subsiding
                  **   **

Amongst the interleavings   Branching downwards
green flesh, olive texture   that we all have becoming
the seeds that the trees   deposit in our lymph
and limbs outstretching   reaching out to touch
            with our eyes for direction
            with our ears for the weaving
              of all singing, swishing
drinking the water, sting of ripeness
                green yet
            sleeping on rocks or against roots
            which hold the land down
the loosening of mist and cascade
Ripples of growth interchange
            in flashes we may enter
              continuous beyond our flickering eyelids
          consents because we imagine
          flowers flourish in the blink of spring
              vines and limbs sag   out in the shadows of
                  summer fragrant evening
sun sprung nettle needles

bark flarings, smolderings sparking
all the stars campfires like ours
that we fiddle and strum
sketch and pour fire

                              the sun seen through leaves
                              vague drops of cool steam
                              the steam takes in gives off

holes in my shoes from pavements
on concrete I work for payment
inside   outside   besides

the joint that passes between all creatures
the cells of air and blood   pass the press of
                                              life to death
the dreams our dreams are dreams of
flags circle, a flap and wave
                    the campfires that the stars become
free of clutter clinging restraint

Compost Heap

Many rocks hold the black plastic down.
            pitch-fork a hole
                for garbage to dissolve in the oozy black depths
Last week it was a chore. I just picked up a corner
surreptitiously to bury what didn't quite fit in so small a hole
guiltily to flap the thin slab of plastic
                back over the bulge.

                    Today I took up
a great swath of cover, and delighted in the feel of each rock,
the warm space about the site, and the voice of
a friend not present then but in the approach to the task
that we shared this time.

Careless Love Canyon

Up Careless Love Canyon, there's a gulch:
dry, called granite bone
that you rise up on through fine sand
                a path through tossed rocks
            Encelia and Creosotebush
        till you reach a climb up
above which the rocks get bigger
and the paths of sand are interrupted
            by massed clumps to clamber over
thickening of the earth bone
            the grass and brush is her hair
                    mattings of it in pits and oozes
the further up you get in Careless Love Canyon
            the closer the
            steepening walls
                    till the trail becomes pure rock
leading through hieroglyphic calligraphies
                    etched in cracks
                        edges meeting nerve channels
        in the atmosphere, aqueous
            and gaseous atoms.

Sitting Upstairs With the Windows Wide Open

Snatching memories that range widely,
I grasp the cypress roots
that clamp onto the cliffs
having a source in the impenetrable
depths of eternity like an old voice that weaves in
collaging fragments of sound
that don't usually make any sense by themselves.

Yet these fragments challenge with ornery arbitrariness
of gesture, where the dance rhythm proceeds from the foot falls.

A grave voice, wet and dark with resonance.
Careful of the splinters and shatter patterns,
clumps of reeds at the mouth of a river,
water hyacinth crowds the water.
Bogart kicks the steam valve that a screwdriver clogged up
because he likes having a machine
that he has to kick to make work.

Tulip in the watershed. Magnolia drifts downstream.
I shall go out into the day, uncross my legs,
and pluck the cobwebs off my eyes,
or just let the wind mat them into a birthplace:
an organic pillow – a sentimental waking into pulse and flesh.

The flowing river of incalculable moments
moved a smooth stone from its bed
kicking up dirt and silt.
Fresh wind enters through the balcony.

No wiser than a beard.   Less white with shorter strands.
Braided beards. Rollicking quilt patches.
Strands of hair bob in the wind before my eyes.
Three wool-clothed hikers high-stepping round a bend
swing their arms in a song of swish.

The point of my pen-shadow,   the shadow of my hand,

overwhelms like phlegm, fleggum my fledgling,
flogging in boll weevil cotton.
O what am I flogging except that it sloshes?
Dear Lisa, my weav'ly wife.

Evil weasel   pen prick   lark spur
lake in pine shadow   gophers, buzzards, beavers,
foenugreek, cardamom, tarragon,
tarry long Talleyrand?   Which direction gliding buzzard?
The burrowing gopher hibernates every night.
The reeds are thick with leeches.
The song of the wool-clothed hikers
wrapped in comic balloon, pulsates
as the light plays on the fog which their breath makes in the cold.

Makes my feet quiver and my head strong,
or else strung with springing.
Clatter of dishes whistling.
Fist swinging clatter of violins: violence that I try to deny
or quality to consent. Air narrows through tubes.
I hear the roar of growth, swift as the wag of a dog's tail.

Editors' note: This is a later version of part of 2-20-68, originally published in
Aldeberan Review #3, no date.

Transmission Linkage

On the dirt road to Hilltop the gear shift jammed between first and second I often had to get out of that car, raise the hood, and pull some levers back that came out of the fire wall. This time I pulled the levers the wrong way. The driveshaft clanked in third. The noise of grinding gears made me drive sixty miles in second. The radiator blew a hose at the end of the road. That was just as well because it snowed a week later and I didn't have antifreeze. When a Havasupai friend suggested using the car, I said that it had a problem with the gears. He proposed helping me fix it, but I didn't know where to begin, and he never had any experience with fixing the gears.

"Let's just drive it until it breaks." Going out in second was slow but sure, if the radiator didn't get too hot. "Does that mean we might have to walk?" This fellow who doesn't even get off his horse in Supai wanted whiskey, but not enough that he would want to walk. He offered me a horse to use for the climb up to Hilltop. He only had two horses. Will would have to stay behind. He wanted to make Will envious. Will hugged his wife and told him that his children might be calling him Daddy by the time we got back. The door would be locked when we returned. He might consider letting us in after he saw what we brought back.

Having a broken-down car was the subject of many amusing conversations about going to town for whiskey, and saved me from actually going. We stayed a few days with an old bachelor who lived in a shack that we helped him to fix, by nailing cardboard that had crated a refrigerator onto his back wall. We used tin can tops to keep the cardboard from coming loose. His roof leaked. It filled a tarp above his bed, which he'd drain off onto the dirt floor when necessary. We helped him fix that too, but he didn't want us to climb on the roof. Only he knew the few safe places to stand. He cooked on a broken kerosene stove and an army surplus mess kit. When his wife died, he threw out all his dishes. He showed us how to make raisin jack, which we drank cloudy after three days fermentation. He knew a place where we could gather clay to sell at the pow-wow as body paint. We could pack it out in tire tubes.

He came back late one night and asked me to write out a story for him. It was a long time before I figured out what happened in order to write an account of it. Early that year he and his brothers were rounding up wild horses on the hilltop. They had fifty head at Dirt Tank, three miles from number five corral. The barbed wire was broken, and fifteen horses got out. They headed them off on a point of the white wall and had their ropes on all of them, including a bay stud with marks in his mane and tail, and white spots on one hind leg. On the way back to Dirt Tank a chestnut mare with a colt whinnied, and the bay stud bolted off. Their horses were too tired to follow. A couple of nights before they spotted the stud in town. The family had been discussing this since. They thought they could get the horse back because it wasn't branded, and they had witnesses to identify the horse. At about this time Will and I left for Hilltop.

We met another camper on the trail who drew a picture on the sand of how the gear shift levers came out of the firewall behind the steering wheel. On the way back up the white wall under the waning moon, I remembered having moved the levers earlier. I poured water into the radiator and fooled around with the transmission linkage, sitting on the fender with a dim flashlight. After a mile I wound out to third, and the gears didn't grind. The radiator stayed cool till we got to the gas station a few miles down the main highway, where I got a new hose.

Either I had put the hose on backwards, or the clamps were worn out. I pulled off of the Grapevine at the first water on the grade from Bakersfield, less than half a minute before the red light came on. I turned the hose around and tightened the clamps. My dog got out of the car during this stop, and I hadn't had him with me for three weeks. I crossed the Grapevine twice that day to look for that bag of bones wrapped in such a fine pelt. It is true he had caused me much inconvenience, traveling with me on the ragged edge, but I sang the saddest song I've every sung on the way back over the Grapevine that day.

The second time across, my muffler started to drag on the ground. I had earlier replaced my muffler with the old straps. One was fairly new, but the older one broke at the top of the pass. I drove the right side onto the curb and then crawled underneath with pliers and wire, holding onto the hot pipe with a rag. The other clamp didn't break for a couple of years. That time I had cut some barbed wire to get onto a dirt road, and my muffler came loose when I wanted to make a quick retreat. The bee-keepers who had spotted us ran to the sheriff to tell him we were either rustling cattle or planting hemp. Luckily a friend of mine was helping him build his garage that day. Unaware that we were the culprits, he nevertheless insisted that the sheriff stay and help him, because he couldn't do that job alone, and the sheriff had promised his aid.

Later that year, I had left my car for a few weeks, and the battery was dead when I got back up to the mountains. I got a jump start from the Washington Ridge bus, but foolishly switched off the engine before I got to town. It wouldn't start on compression down a steep hill with a truck pushing it. After two and a half days on the charger, the battery got the car started but went down overnight. I was planning on driving to Berkeley to attend a curry party, but I was broke and decided to hitch—hike to Chico to work in the almonds. First I would bathe in the Yuba. On the way to the swimminghole on the dirt road, I got a ride all the way to Berkeley in time for the party.

From there I got a ride to Chico with Will. I knocked the almond branches with a long bamboo pole after the shaker went thru. A few days later I had enough for a new battery and an oil change. The Washington Ridge bus gave me another jump start, and I went down to Grass Valley. I was changing my oil in a vacant lot when an old man ran out to complain. I nervously started to put the oil back in without tightening the drain plug. Down on my knees I tightened the oily nut before it all drained out. I managed to get all the oil in, air filter back on, trash and tools put away, and all I left behind was a can-opener.

In Susanville my exhaust pipe off the manifold developed a crack. I tried some heat sealing tape, which smelled like rubber burning under the hood whenever I did any climbing. Eventually the tape peeled off. I took the exhaust pipe out to have it welded. I forgot to keep the flange on the pipe, which fell off when the two pieces came apart. I had to work the flange on from the other end.

Earlier, when I had installed the muffler I had the benefit of a grease rack and an air chisel. In my exuberance with the air chisel I tore a hole in the exhaust pipe, which didn't need to be replaced at that time. Along with the muffler came two metal sleeves. One of these fit the pipe and covered the hole. The muffler was moved back three inches, which were critical in fitting the hangers to the clamps under the car. The way that I had hung the muffler caused a persistent rattle from the tail pipe bouncing between the rear axle and the leaf spring. The sleeve that I had put on prevented me from getting the flange back onto the pipe.

I hammered a chisel into the pipe until I remembered that the pipe had a hole in it anyway. I sawed off the sleeve, measured the pipe, walked to a muffler shop with the dimensions (which would also stop the rattle by moving the muffler closer to the original clamps). The two pieces would not fit together, however. I had to drive with the pipe disconnected from the muffler down the back streets to a shop where they got it together with a blow torch. I had so many problems with the exhaust system that I finally got enough practice to try to bluff my way into a job at a muffler shop in Paso Robles.

Baling wire is handy for temporary measure. U-clamps can't be torqued too tightly. The straps that parts houses sell don't always fit. I had an IH Scout with sixteen inch tires that were really high off the ground. The expensive strap at the International parts house didn't fit, and neither did the universal. I tore the strap off at the rivet and bolted it to a piece of the original assembly to put it at the right angle. That gave me a lot of satisfaction.

Junkyards have always interested me, or old wrecks in wild places that have started to blend with their surroundings, like the wreck with rust patterns at the top of Topocoba, which affords occasional shelter, or down by the Susan River there are two well rusted truck bodies. The hobos in Nogales can be found in the junkyard, occupying comfortable cars which used to run. One time, in order to be alone, I sought out a junkyard in Huntington Beach, climbed over the fence and found a Studebaker with recliner seats. I once advised a friend with a junk truck cluttering his parking lot to find someone who delights in getting old useful vehicles running again, like Peeler, who got the oral transmission from Stokes himself, on Oakie Shade Tree mechanical work.

On muddy roads out near Forest Ranch, we had Jack's four wheel drive '47 Dodge pickup, and we tried to make a thirty-six Dodge pickup run. We siphoned out the old gas, pulled the plugs, squirted Marvel Mystery Oil down the valve chambers, taped the exposed wires, fiddled with the points, and pulled it around on a tow chain. It started up a couple of times going down a steep hill, but wouldn't stay running on the level, so I towed it back. I didn't have to go back up the steep hill we went down, but once we had started, Peeler accepted the challenge. I lost compression slowing down for a turn and started a mudslick. The more the wheels spun, the harder it was to get up. There was no way to back down around that curve, it being such a steep grade. We had two trucks stuck together on a towchain, and I needed to keep the wheels moving slowly enough to get traction, without killing the engine with the extra weight it was hauling. Peeler would shout abuse and instruction up to me in the towcar: how I shouldn't shift on the slip, even if I lugged it. The rubber from our tires warmed up the mud before we reached the top. I had to lug it past the slick.

Lugging a diesel can severely damage the lifters. I have learned to play the diesel like a musical instrument. I run a Cummings Six, 10 wheel Ford, which used to belong to an Italian antipasto cannery in New Jersey. My tenderest toe touch accelerates it just enough to make the hill and to keep my distance. Nobody has bothered to fix the short on the oil pressure sender. If I ever over-rev or lug the engine, the red light on the dash flashes a warning. I have gotten so that I can run to Santa Clara without seeing that light.

Six pistons slap and patter at 30 cycles per second at the beginning of a shift. After it accelerates 10 cycles faster, I fit the shift lever into a groove, or pull out the split-axle button. With the precision of a chord change, the rear end meshes with a gear that has more teeth. Accompanied by a gentle, steady acceleration, the wheels start spinning faster. If I am going at the same speed as the rest of the traffic, I hold it down to 35 cycles per second. For a hill I need to wind out to a few more cycles of torque.

When I chant from my belly to the same pitch as the six pistons slap, this venerable truck sounds as beautiful as a creek rapids.

For a long time the seal on the air brakes was bad, which made them lock up. In order to release them, I had to build up the air pressure, flip up the emergency brake lever, and get out of the truck. Under the frame, between the right rear tandem wheels, I used to stick my thumb over the hole where air was rushing out. When I heard the highest pitch of air escaping, I took my thumb off of the hole and run for the cab to get a hand or a foot on the brake. After I had to conduct this ritual on South Van Ness one time, I learned how to release the brakes without getting out of the cab. With the same foot on the brake and the accelerator, I built the air pressure back up, and gunned the engine a few more seconds. Thus I got out of a few tight situations, but I'm certainly glad that the company finally had the seal fixed.

I once spent the night of my birthday in the back of an abandoned gas station in San Bernardino, right above the Interstate, stuck on the onramp with two other resourceful hitch hikers. We borrowed a broom and cleaned it up, turned a sign over to make a platform, and found some rugs and cardboard to soften it. All night long the trucks were shifting down for the grade. On the desert side, a drunk Chicano in a Toyota asked me to drive, and told me that I was a tramp; anybody could tell that; and that was good. Over the years he has been able to find the most dependable companeros, by picking up tramps on the road. "I've got to go home now, but tomorrow we can go to New Mexico, you and I and my old lady. Just tell her you work with me at the Rohr plant. My people will take you in." He drilled me with the short answers I was to give to the questions his family might ask. He wanted me to floor it on the downhill stretches: "When I used to be a pilot." We bought some hundred proof Grandad in China Lake, and I headed down for Mojave. "Where did you get that ring?" It was given to me by a friend in Point Reyes. He got it from Danny Simplicio, a Zuni silversmith who got the stone from the Four Corners area of New Mexico. "Just say Four Corners, that's all you need to say. They are from New Mexico."

I am usually inclined towards the longer and more detailed response, but he was informing me about how to survive around the people he knew. When talk is finally out there for me to ride, I betray the slovenliest habits of intellect and disdain any lack of detail I might possibly consider. Some people might only see that I was using some words they didn't understand and meandering from brush to bramble in my rambling aimless talk with continuous complication, following digressions which leave the main current of expression behind. I can remember when I was a flash in the pan, exulting in my discoveries when people understood more than mere talk, which only imperfectly conveys the jump from axon to dendron. The island feels the reverberation of the wave deep within its volcanic center. Sometimes I'm chagrined at the inabilities I manifest. People consider me incapable of the deep sentiments they possess, a witless non-sequitur from doubtless subterranean origin. Others are delighted with my nonsensical musings and feel my waves beyond the shores of their skin, deep within their volcanic centers. They look with wonder at one who blithely blunders in a brash froth of talk.

Unpublished Work of Lowell A. Levant

Enkidu

The courtesan found him roaming in a meadow
and tempted him away from the herd
                        lying on a grassy knoll
her knee up
her back arched
her belly smooth ridged
her cunt flowing with juices

Driven to her by the smell
following with his eyes
the curves from her thighs
to the valley of her neck   he longed
to pull away her gold and purple flowing veils, to
run his hairy arms over her olive gray lines

He roared and stormed and clasped her shoulders tight
found her tender notch and screamed
chilled and warmed, exploding in the rhythm
spilling out in laughs, gasps, roars:
Mirth and sober overpowering ecstasy
springing exhaustion.

                        She clung to me so desperately
                        I thought she was dying
                        I moved from side to side
                        and caressed her
                        Then I felt her belly soften
                        her clenched teeth loosen

I stood on my hind feet and walked to a great rock.
The beasts I roamed with were gathered watching me.
I ran down to them to tell them what I knew
how they could stand on their hind legs too.

They turned away and I walked back
to hold the woman in my arms.

March 1967

Slipping a Shade Below

In the shadows of the woods across the river textures beckon
The wings of hidden band-tailed pigeons
flap within the branches

Ministering to the unspoken needs
of his comrade,   the personal shaman, <u>Cacoat</u>
sits upon the further crags of a butte cliff
just above the low-lying clouds.
He pays no particular regard
to any source of light, and looks no further
than the sight can trace all around this place.

Dark spirits beyond the shadows
make it known to me what I see
Come hither under this tree.
I hear and sing the same signals.
The downwind drives a struggling buzzard across boundaries
to the harbor that stretches over storms
like a limp band.
Smothering the fetters of memories and habits,
the complexity dodges the ticket taker
and sneaks under the bleachers.
While the whirligig spins
my pencil pushes across the thin line
of its sharp point, tracing the foundation
of a safer refuge.
Thankful, wondrous, sick with failure, opening my guts,
I let my voice lift up what's left of my aspirations.

He also wrote aesthetic treatises of great complexity.
He energetically participated in the common work
        and did not consider what was his share
        or the task be menial.

Stoned at The Bialy's with Robert Kelley

Ah I know why you
    keep your head down when you listen
know why I'd keep
      my face turned to blankness
      that all my senses be channeled
thru dark chartreuse tunnels, lined
      with cashmere, fur, and velvet
where the lines are clear of the pattern
distilled to colorless blazing fluid
filled with broad clouds of generating friction
      where there's fog there's warmth
      you will find when you least expect
      where you least expect to look, chug-a-jug
          of luck, gang bang, cuckoo
          shell-lack-luster

Maha-Mudra:
(to flow and to feel a part of everything
    rather than to follow or to lead, as if one
    were somehow separate from other beings)
Two new friends have bid me welcome in their midst.
One of them objects to my obvious faults. I have no quarrel
with these meritorious criticisms, of which I am not the
exclusive object. In my quest for greater understanding I may have
attained my goals imperfectly, but my direction is sure, and I'm
attempting to rectify the matters as soon as I conclude my other
projects.

The Sweetness

The sweetness of broken resolutions accumulates gently
within the traps of habitual enunciation.
Abject objects: tug of war over things
Objection, anger makes me want to throw away
the compass and the map I've brought with me
to pursue the goal, to give up!
Friction of resistance, the noise
that the belch makes as it passes through the throat.
Hair follicles, mucous lumps, and paddles of flapping skin
get in the way, tug on the gas, cling to the rush singing out.

How many times I've given up to a force pushing past
The dust blows up in a low cloud bubble
yellow from the glow of the sun.
Sparkles of dustlets strike off the major globe.
Fixedly watching the failure bomb out
I listen to the song I could have met headlong
if I knew we'd merge. I've been picked up
by the force pushing past, which seems to give a tug
that pulls me up to attention.
I feel the wind outside before the wind inside.
Homage to the bottom we touch in common.
It moves up just as fast as the force we exert
to stand up to it, to put it forth instead of throwing it off.
I ache certainly, yet so much more by exiting from the excitement
than to wallow in the mudhole muddle
where I try to think I'm mellowing.

Letter to Doug & Ruth & Tad

Your sparrows pecking make cricket sounds.
seed gathering?
scattering; human respect
is improving, the posture of the pecking
birds is awkward, the wildflowers
are upside down, on top of a hill.
The seeds float uphill.

In Gentle Lust

Froth: the first child of Water and Air
deposits silt and wears away rock   .
        go to the sea's edge at dawn
        stand between two great rocks
        endure the waves upon your bare chest:
                                sudden sea slap bearing soft froth
                                bringing sun wind rain to earth
                                regulating the course of the moon
What are stars but specks of froth?

november morning / not yet light
rode my bike into golden gate park
onto an island of favorite lake
swans and ducks waking and going onto the water
fine sand packed tight at the island's shore
trails moving up into the center
still / brown water / blinding rhododendron bushes on
the opposite shore / and the buildings of the medical center
circling the island i re-crossed the bridge and found myself at
the crossing of the main park drive riding at full speed
                then stopping to sit
                        on dew wet grass overlooking a buffalo meadow
hunched thick shoulders, busy cocks / stepping slow / firm
a few buck deer in the eucalyptus
        further on the road / the sea – reaching into darkness
when the distance brightened: a tall rainbow
the mane of a dark horse changing color with the day coming
                sandpipers playing near to drowning at the shore
moved on. later a friend told me there's a rainbow at every sunrise
you simply have to look the other way .

FOR MOM

With Love And Appreciation.
For the colors of L'ESTAQUE
to dance out and make you tingle
the swaying trees at LES COLLETTES
to lull you with undulant colors
For new faces to emerge from the
LUNCHEON OF THE BOATING PARTY
And the flowers in the BOUQUET BEFORE A MIRROR
I hope will awaken the colors outside
this book also – rolling out of slumber
For the rainbow to appear in mist
that the sun broke through a spot
        across the sky

Lalo

14 February 1969

For Caren

I Give you
a sprig of
mistletoe —
for you to kiss
        under
for you for
        you to kiss
I give a kiss
        under the
                mistletoe
for you for
the mistletoe
Lovely Caren

— LALO

If you don't know, Why do you Ask?

Abundance clogs the pipes, and pays the scoundrels back
who would want others to have less
tangled in their unreleased beneficence.
Grease dries to tar. The resins float away in the rain.
Cleans, cools and lubricates only when in continual flux.

The pure waters empty in with the garbage and salt.
Even if I can stay wiser by treading the narrow creeks,
I can't follow them to their source
before they dwindle to nothing, preternaturally calm
in the eye of the storm, trapped and flanked by furies as ideas springing
forth.

I would rather mingle within greater waters
and after a short happy interval
lose every advantage I'd gained,
float off and forget how I began to move down again
with pure water. I remember falling
all split up in drops. Did I ever land?

On the moss of a black oak
with three or four hundred other drops
split off from their fellow travelers.
Before we could get acquainted, the pulp sucked us down
to the roots where we met a battalion of ground water drops.
We slipped behind them and seeped into streaming channels of excess,
Riding down with old friends by now.

I can never rest from nerves
They just travel at such diverse speeds
whether I'm with it or totally zonked out.
I throw these lines out and hold on
till the wind or water weight tugs of fish or kite
The line just slumps unless there's tension upon it.
I think any looseness will pull from behind in ephemeral ways.

Crust of water: green brown fuzz
flies and gnats: stagnation.

The wind blows over a crust of growth
and makes it swirl and spiral up to a cone
that covers the earth, showers lumps of moss
that take hold upon rocks and wear into them
to split them apart and to make them shatter, erode away
A great deal of noise zooms up and crumbles in to clods.
What's left of the gloomy cone arouses yellow dust clouds.

Why am I so?

the fog doesn't burn
away, but it's
warm out of the wind.
walking thru the
grass, crickets were
hopping, the elusive
textures that fog
weaves, on the
headlands –

The look you give
me, is it the
same as the way
I see myself

You are watching
me from the perspective
of having overcome
some faults that I'm
still beleaguered with,
& with the look
of wonder at one
who blithely blunders
without seeming to
consider basic strategic
importance, & yet
comes out structuring
everything in a
manner you couldn't
contrive

Winter Work

I grabbed the cold gas pump nozzles
       in the morning fog
kneeled on shop rags to search
for the points on the frame
to prop the jacks on the lift
to flip the levers or
squeeze grease into zerts
till the boots popped.

One morning I thrived on gunk and messes
cleaned up the oil drain can on rollers
that leaked out the sides from being overfilled.

      It made me not want to tell beautiful stories
       about going down into the belly of the earth.
Making gradual transitions, I buried the bent roots
of walnut trees in a valley field
and pulled out the marking stakes after they got planted.
Three days of hard work don't drive me to desperate spend-thriftiness:
"A glass of whatever they're drinking for everybody in the house."
or other rash extravagance.

2-72

The Wheels and Gears of Beauty

A chain of perceptions turns the mind around.
The teeth mesh which harness faculties of perception
to efficient productive labor. The team of horses
and the 10 spoked wheel move the freight
from dock to rack or surplus, from pony to pallet
to the bed of a trailer, across the grimy road
to the next dock plate, where all the raw and packaging
materials for industrial use get brought in and used up.
At the big places there's usually a logjam of truck receiving.
At the shipping end, the clock turns out the work.
The demands of production determine when the stock runs out.
For a man with imagination to tie up with a high pressure outfit
in a unique indispensable manner truly obligates the fullest attention,
so that the teeth grow sharp which lends to production,
and the teeth which transform an everyday situation into
a meaningful and moving involvement with the least disruption
of the natural pattern growing sharp in the absence
of such an involvement.

A Poet Drives a Truck

Transmit and reflect light with a steady glow.
      Inspect the equipment routinely and thoroughly.
Explore alternate routes when feasible.
      Let the eyes range over the land, the sky,
the near, the distant road, and the mysterious
peripheries.
Transcend rage and panic with humor and consideration.
      Tell the truth especially when a brilliant lie
seems more appropriate.
Look flowers in the eyes.
      Frisk about like a dog unbound.
Sniff the night perfume of trees.
      Listen to the songs of birds.
Let them take wing in the breath and soar forth
to the moon.

Editors' Note. This poem, from which this volume takes its name, was published circa 1999 in a newsletter published by Lowell's employer at the time, titled "Still Manifesting."

Ode to my Father

A keen business-manager and a skilled pressman organized his working areas for safety and efficiency and kept his printing presses and other equipment clean and well oiled. Talented with arithmetic he often amazed me with the results of a calculation before I could find a piece of paper.

Through the 1950's up until 1964 he owned and operated a job-printing business in Huntington Park, CA. I looked forward to going with him to the print shop on Saturdays when I was ten or twelve. He taught me a few simple tasks and took me out for lunch at George's Bar-B-Que. He went on Boy Scout trips with me to the Los Padres Mountains and encouraged me to recount the adventures we had.

On Sunday drives with the family he would break out into a free song to express his pleasure in the beautiful surroundings with his deep baritone voice. My own interest in jazz and extemporaneous—ecstatic—ad—lib—scat—singing began with those outbursts of his.

Very much a morning person he was usually the first one up: to put on coffee, to go outside to greet the sky, to play with the dog, to do his chores cheerfully, and to sing a playful song. In the last fifteen years we have played many cribbage and domino games together. He always challenged me to see beyond the immediate hand. He encouraged me to seek steady employment and to invest in secure housing.

When he came with my Mom to visit me in Newark, I usually got involved in fixing and cleaning something which I hadn't gotten around to doing in the last minute flurry of activity before their arrival. He was generous with his "know how" and understood the principle of sleeves, pins, rivets, & other esoteric devices besides nuts, bolts, and screws. I miss my cribbage partner and adviser. I remember him slicing the standing rib roasts with his freshly sharpened knife.

He took us out to fine restaurants when I was a child: Welch's, Robaire's, Felipe's, and Olvera Street for taquito's.

He loved the fresh air of the ocean. He took us for walks on the piers, kibitzing with fishermen about their catches or bait. He went for walks with me in Point Mugu State Park and let me teach him purple sage, black sage, coreopsis, buckwheat, chemise, mountain holly, ceanothus, encelia.

Wherever he walked he was willing to say Hello to fellow sojourners. Everybody in the neighborhood knew him, kids especially. He was that kind of guy. I'm not the only one who will miss him – not by a long shot.

A Visit near Bald Peak

Will did some palm reading after dinner.
Giancarlo asked me if I could do that.
I replied, "I have studied it somewhat.
It has a scientific basis. The chiromancer
needs to ask whether the subject has had any
hand injuries or diseases in order to eliminate
erroneous diagnoses."

"Moreover the palm reader gleans a lot of
The information psychically from the subject
This is not a mystery. Mind reading is commonplace
The major impediment to reading minds is
not having a clear and receptive mind.
The work that my friends have done in meditation
has helped them to get rid of thoughts that get
in the way of truly listening to other beings
Another friend meditates to understand the
plants in his garden. I can sometimes hit the dock
with one stroke and make smooth gear shifts."

" Animals don't need to talk to each other to
understand the group's objectives. A tribe
close to the basis of survival needs little
discussion. Language has the disadvantage
of distancing people from each other
Will and I used to say 'Telepathy is not a
gift but a condition of friendship'."

August 2009

Editors' Note: This was Lowell's last poem, written in Portland, OR.

Untitled Poems

(untitled)

The sun has gone down on the swimminghole
I lay upon a rock that's still warm
The old men's sweat song ripples in the rapids
The last batch of home brew tastes better every
    nite the bottles have a chance to age.
I cut down a steep hill with felled logs
to clamber over, crossed the creek, and
started up the other side, thinking I'd be
out of the diggins by crossing the creek
I climbed up mighty high and could see
the remaining light in the west dim
When I looked over the other side I saw
a steep cut of red earth on each side
of a mined valley
I could make it down easily enough but it
would be quite a chore getting up over the
left cliff which hung over loose dirt
where I'd lose ground
I turned back down the hill cut around
it, and finding a trail thru Manzanita made
it back up to Whittlesea land at the
edge of Brofey Meadow at
the very same point that another trail
starts on the other side of the dug valley.
Whew
which some friends who came over
the night before showed me

(untitled)

I've ranged over meadows
fragrant with lingering wildflowers
& grasslands getting toasted bright
with caterpillars dropping from liveoaks

The fresh wind in the shade of a rock cleft
so downwind that deer woke me
by poking their muzzles
into my magical site.
         They blew out the candle
I'd set in the granite metate
which kept the mosquitoes away
while I dozed Salinan
ancestors ground the ghosts of acorns

There is no internal continuity with
the side of me that is easily influenced
by other people
but occasionally the spark of
originality finds some leftover fuel
slightly burnt around the campfire
in the morning
With special people that I relate with
deeply I can get carried away
with more than just
what I'm putting out
but a melding of that – flow
not even broken up by distance
but certainly helps to be close
for it to happen

*Editors' Note: This is an earlier version of "Stump Top Doctoring," published in
Coyote Run.*

(untitled)

the candle flame as steady as the
            gulping glorious warm fragrant bath
    of concentration in common
            ferment of kinship
    long remembered rhythms/that we were lounging
            on the thick carpeted cloud forests
        sunrays streaming in patterns suggesting
arches and bridges of cottages, palaces
        waterfalls and gulches
        vulture riding the same wind
                passing thru, observing the routes
                our images set

(untitled)

The deciduous trees have graced the hill
with green and the grass
is ready to flower
Poppies, brodeia, and ceanothus
are fully blooming
The wrens & titmice chirp from the
newly budded blue oak.
The shade of green I see but
once a year

April 3

(untitled)

The escarpment of the
desert mountains
levels of shadow &
outcropped rock zig Zag

I wondered if there were
a melody interwoven
in these patterns

I formed a graph
in my mind
to correspond to
musical notes

& began to hear the
music that their shade
cast to my eyes

their shapes moved

(untitled)

The rap is the folding over of the bubbling
        is the wrap of blossoming
seed spreading with rapid growth
as fast as a synapse
        electric seeds boiling
        to make tea— seed food
soiled cabbage grows wild like any weed
        malva growing out back that I'll cook with spinach
because I want to taste from soil I've pissed on
threw garbage, beer cans, wine bottles
and now drying a kelp horn that looks like a cobra

Yesterday morning the mist did spring
        in the hill crevices
then it got hot and fog lay out
on the Bay - making the Golden Gate golden

they tell me who were in the hills
        the smell from either my kelp horn
        or the piss that's clung to the boards
        of the balcony made me move
        the shaded cobra out to the sun
        presumably to dry

Fly describing irregular multigon
the clouds of my smoke over it
as the clouds clear/ rises from the plane it held
        whilst I observed
it moves up now but that's like a mistake
a side of the multigon
that wasn't the right draft or light
so back to three feet above the floor
        those are curves the fly is describing – as I
        dumb scribe – dump cough
        describe rather than fold, bubble
        blossom, boil, toil and
        cough out radiant smoke
        make the fly stoned
dumb scribe – content to await the moment when I shall

speak this rosy and warm with the calm which envelopes
                    and folds
            with my lips I seal
            the rhythms/ let them slip
            up and down the stairs of my throat
knobby shit – slide down the banister
and be buggered or crazed
                    better to climb a greased pole or wallow
                    with the pigs in moist tender swamplets
                        with wild pigs that don't stink
                        because they eat well
When there's slime, loll
strenuous movement is occasioned only
when the ooze is lost
            the past is present
            cool dry air blows thru the throat
                to wake the yawn
            or the tautness melts weary
            the chin folds, eye lashes quiver

The movements of the fly seem jerky
and I doubt that its home's in the air
Then what about those electric seeds
simmering and flashing under my skin
involuting multi-angularly
                    on the goggles
                    once having brought them
                    to a boil, turn the fire
                    the river will set
                    slightly lower and lower
                    the sun-bow soon
            at home in slime, sea, rain
            wind takes getting used to
sun-bone, the skeleton of the earth
vijnana alaya: the memory of our seed spreading
            flashing interactions
gushing over the rainbow falls
into the lake of   day
like the sea waves/ wear out gorges
            crash and drain from rock
                    eroding the skeleton

to let live things grow
I have felt the pulse of a mountain
with my fingering roots seeking moist dirt
that pulse is the mountain sinking
growth exudes from its folds
    from water, and shadow
        once having brought the water
       to a boil, turn the fire
      slightly lower and lower

24 February 1968

(untitled)

I don't know whether I'll ever become
other than the moth I am
        braving the candle fire, dis-
regarding the open window
        with the draft that makes the candle
flutter   I folly my shivers out
following against the chilly current
making it out by bass awkward luck
with the legs of a jackrabbit
the ears of a sparrow
           (just chirruping now
        for the first time
        the window's purple
        half moon up still bright
the eyes of a fish
the teeth of an anteater
        (The leafless tree has pink branches
        above the sloping gray roof
        of the green stucco
arms the front paws of a Kangaroo Rat
tongue of a cow mooing

I have claws I only use on myself
when I run up against
     a block in the path
        (or pink clouds across from the sun
         ripe oranges in the tree outside
         amber whiskey half way up
         the folds inscribed on the low
part/ of the glass
        clods of spongy lime and clay
        roll down behind me as I turn
     pull a handkerchief from my pocket
     snap it into the air
     draw it in front of my nose
     and forget which direction I was heading
stumbling backwards over the boulders
duck head in, land on shoulders
and roll baby roll

I hang upside down like a bat
or a sloth with three toes
        with the voice of a tree toad
        I call up to the ground
                    down to the sky
croaking, toking, drinking
pushing the glass away
for calling too much attention to itself
            I would have left for work by now
            having stayed up the night
            but my boss Louise drove over at 6
            switched me to this afternoon
            I only have to worry about lasting till 12
        everything back asswards
only sometimes comes back as words
nothing every sunrise
anything... only someplace!
could take the form of a silver horn
or a plumbeous gnatcatcher
                    in the filigreed tree
        (often   just a movement in the chakras
        caught in the quavering throat
        or the ping in the belly
                    that floods the brain
                (my persistence at bringing
                    the emptying glass closer
belly button of a snail
hips of a saddle
        to fit on a sea horse
whale spout, pelican
the arch of frothy waves.

27 January 1970

(untitled)

How's about stalking off into a sidekick four-step
clink of can. Strip the means of their sounds.
He inherited a brand new isosceles television set
for only sending into the daily mirror a strip of hair,
borne infrequently by the wind, but usually requiring a clipper.

Sometimes she just lets us loose upon her downy fluff.
Hillocks of alliteration for strangulation of aforesaid requirement
designed to be reducible to an even lower frequency
which switches up if it is of an odd disposition.
So seldom does he pick up his post that the dead letters
are starting to smell. Could you ask him to shift his weight to the other
shoe?
He doesn't know any better and is on the other side of the heater
right now, so give him what worthwhile forgiveness will allow.
It certainly does wonders for the countenance. Besides what near
and far phenomena are circling below the ear cylinders.
He made a jest of it. Take me now
So that I can last the whole night
without kicking it all off.

14/II/71

(untitled)

Without any expectation of reward
or desire to return to any balance, disappointment betrays me anyway.
I watch the log, and the saw strews sawdust out of the cut.
Be not ungenerous my honey. The fewer faretheewells I get
the more I expect, yet if I do not address you disrespectfully.
Behind that veil drawn over your face, your eyes watch me flounder
without your support. Allowing you the freedom to disappear,
I peer about with sharp eyes like a tiger with insatiable craving
in every other possible direction than the effect of your speaking to me
while I speak. Allow me to ascend. O magic Tortoise.

14/II/71

(untitled)

So characteristic of me to blunder into the mistake a friend warned me
specifically to avoid.
Fooling around in bed one morning I bragged about spiritual prowess.
I wanted to be honest instead of entertaining and ended up being neither
when she asked me questions I didn't feel right answering
about the conversations I could hear without being close enough to make out
what was being said, and the music I could imagine from the radio across the
street that only when I walked outside could I actually hear.
She wondered whether I could hear conversations that were going on inside a
house when the doors were closed. I said I could, and that made it seem
like I had a special gift that I did nothing to maintain and didn't really deserve:
a skill for getting deeper into feelings that emanate from places
to know someone and to be in his house, to remember knowing someone
similar and to see him talking at a distance in a bar.
I could reconstruct the talk by inference from the snatches of conversation
and unconscious play from the subliminal noise and feelings I got.

When she asked me how I accomplished this, I made something up
because I wasn't in the same sensitive place where the imagination
operates so effectively.   I said I could feel the feeling,
keep it with me and gradually focus in on more specific fragments
until I had the whole conversation going on when I wasn't even paying
attention, and now I'm bored with it and don't want to hear what I pick up
without trying.
I avoid the impressions, and they pursue me.
She said, "Why do you put yourself down so much," and I was merely trying
to take out the sting of myself congratulation for having such wonderful
mysterious powers that I did nothing to maintain.
What I said didn't seem like such an awful story at the time.
That was the way many another relationship fell to dust.

10/73

(untitled)

I'm considered a nut by several people independently here at the hospital
because I ask them if they can help me think up a name for my pet gnat
or introduce them to Moe the mop bucket and encourage him to smile
by pulling the wringer arm down, drawing the mouth where the mop wrings out.
They wait til I'm out of earshot before they laugh at my jokes

I'm truly slipping, as I predicted walking back to the stageline on Humbug Road
I sleep more than I need to just in order to have some entertaining dreams
For example the other day I dreamt there was a hole in the cardboard skirt around
the engine of my car. I stuft a rag into it and drove to Santa Monica on the freeway
I drove into a shop where I met some of my high school friends.
I decided to take the skirt off the engine, to the applause of everyone there.
Once I had removed it we all spread it out flat.

It became a swimming pool, & I was feeling up Ann Gerchic, who was the prettiest
chick in the 9th grade but nobody would ask her out because we all thot
she was otherwise committed. She was friendly to me but I never asked her out.
Those were the thoughts in my mind as I was feeling her bulging tits under
the swimming suit she was wearing, ah so tenderly.
We all started going off the diving board, which turned into my erect cock,
and started to piss into the pool, awakening me to the urgency of a full bladder

(untitled)

The primary prayer of the Jewish people is "Shma Yisrael
Adonai Elohenu, Adonai Echod." A rough literal translation
would be "Hear 0 Israel; the lord our God; the lord is one!"
I quibble with the concept of lord because it implies a male
hierarchy in a stratified society. I would also extend the
territory to include all life forms on the earth. "Listen
earth people; God has revealed the way to us; there is one God!"
In the Fifth Century B.C. when the Old Testament was rewritten,
there were a plethora of Gods and Goddesses and considerable
confusion over ethical conduct. One God meant one law: The Torah:
The Golden Rule, The Ten Commandments, and the history of a tribe
to whom God revealed Himself. Not everyone would interpret the law
the same way. Chapter 71 of the Tao Te Ching begins, "Not knowing
that one knows is best; thinking that one knows when one does
not know is sickness..." Truth and justice are always beyond
individual perspectives. No one can explicitly formulate general
truths. The Navaho's greet each other with the expression "Go
in Beauty: May Beauty Surround You." For them Justice is a form
of Harmony. With these eclectic considerations I submit this prayer.

Listen to the song of the weather, the seasons, and the
hum of life. Watch the textures in the web; smell the odors; and
dance to the rhythms. No one can say exactly how each life entwines
with the whole fabric. All earth creatures must obey one evanescent
law. The highest worship is to transmit one's own vision to others.
One serves God best by seeing beyond one's limited perspective
and listening to other creatures, including those who cannot
talk human languages.

Telepathy flourishes in the absence of speech. The further
away one gets from civilization, the louder the landforms speak.
I pray for guidance, not to influence the course of events. When
my own thoughts have calm wisdom born of a higher perspective,
my higher power is speaking to me. When my dreams point out the
futility of my current activities or the possible new directions
my life can take, I am listening to my higher power.

2 March 1995

Poems about Lowell A. Levant

3 Aug 1971, Waiting at the Mediterraneum for Bean and Lowell

by Kenneth Irby

To Sonoma County yesterday, visiting Mike and Pam Ross to pick up
Lowell's records— homebrew and notebooks under the apricot trees
— pigs and sheep, chickens, dogs — big garden on one side, and the
layers of distance set by the eucalyptus on the hills showing depths
through as if cliff precipices sighted, continually ticked with the wind-
shifted leafshimmer— the great meat soul bird with teeth — foxy
poisonous women invoked — "what do you remember of what you've
written, and how long afterwards? —news of Chico and of carpenter's
work (Mike an apprentice) — "I want some kind of head work I can
fall back on if I get hurt, if my hands get hurt, a carpenter depends on
his hands, I can *plan,* you know, like when I got that splinter in my
thumb, but I need something I can fall back on and make money at if I
can't work like I am now" — Bromige's analytical mind—red
printer's/binder's clothbound dummy blank page note-book now filled
— "I finished my first book and started on another one"— sceptre 4
foot onion stalk, bulb to crown of florets, shaft swelling like an
eriogonum inflatum-deflatum —"Pam and I eat about 2 cloves of garlic
apiece every day" — "did you walk out back to the Frontier?" "yeah, up
that hill? get a good view of the freeway, whiff of smog" "yeah!"
laughter beyond humor, belly relaxer— comings and goings of dogs:
Rosebud, Rosie, Rose (Bean), Tulpa (Lowell), Rodeo (Mike) — "there's
a lot in your notebook about sheep slaughtering— you've done your
own" "I hit the sheep over the head with a hammer then cut their
throats — I slaughtered 6 sheep for this guy and he gave me one"
"what're you gonna do with the pigs?" "well, Portia's a brood sow, not
for meat—I'll probably keep one of the little ones when they're big
enough" "shoats" "what're their names" "their names? one of them's
called_____ , and one's_____ , and the others' names
are pork and *bacon"*— "I like to work about 6 hours and then quit around
1 or 2 you know, rest, sleep a few hours, talk or read, have a little dinner
and then go back to work — I've been working 12 hours a day that
way—you know, all jobs in America ought to be like that, knock off in
the middle of the day like a siesta" — in the field below
the other house, a swaybacked bony horse and a sad quiet burro —
Mike at work with his friend on that other house, ripping up boards,
putting in a new kitchen — we left by 4, 4:30, back down the deadend

road, Penn Grove to Cotati, to find and say goodbye to another friend, she not at home, Bean played "Joy Spring" on the piano, and Couperin's "Les barricades mysteriéux"— Lowell left a note for Joanna and talked with her tall blonde roommate who came in and wondered who we were— and then back to Berkeley, stopping in Vallejo at Toney's Bar and Package Goods, across the alley from the Greyhound bus depot, for dime beers and cheese twists, eyeing the array of cheap liquor, and sandwich signs—old gentlemen, black and white and filipino, having Old Grandad at 35¢ a shot with dime beer chasers — "are you going back to the Philippines this year?" — white-panama'd whitehaired white gentleman to white panama'd filipino gentleman — "no, I went back last year" "to see your children?" — back into the cool of Berkeley and the Bay after the Coast Range inner valley heat — the slope of time, a day at a time, August's fall slant across the apricot shaded grass stubble—the clarity of our days slipping with us, filling the great inner lake of accumulation

Strawberry Canyon Poem
by Kenneth Irby

We followed the fire road up into the hills
for night time's sake, for smells of jasmine and of amaryllis
the faintest light register on the side bush growth
ceanothus? I said to Lowell would cover
most of any guesses what
not for the unaccounted registers of recollection, not
of tabulation *whose*
                        Lowell for the
distance from those lights of the Rad Lab and chicken farm
still lit our way
                  and I was off for
any, stripping off my shirt
till the mosquitoes
                sensuality
of unintended impingements
                        trying
incorrectly as we argued and I lost
to place *this*
pace along *this*
fire road
with all the other times
a *here* that is the mappist's
fixed by what should be the necessary
lineaments of growing things
that nonetheless follow no
and will not be described by a
                        Sheer memory
the greatest adjunct only if
more important attentions
are incessantly at work
                The path
back by the quickest
weight of the rut in the dark
only the feet to the contour worn
by the same
suspended searching blind
and certain as the vine
But it's clear our

               (two, for Lowell
went first down the path
the last stretch)
                   way is polysemous
remembered and at
the fingers and the words
renerved

We Might Say Poetry
by Kenneth Irby

We might say poetry
as accumulation of specific
but instead we talked about the mind
's a sixth sense, the Tibetans'
sense of it

        West in the mist
Tamalpais' top floated
the earth that was not connected
was ours clear up to the hillside
where Alexandra David-Neel spoke in Lowell
the scatterings of trees
on hills like our own hill
unpredictable
           "the dovetailing
or interlacing of ridges
              no line on a map

can represent"

but the greenery of grass
is fence

cutting even the heart away
with the brightness of the day

SW towards Orinda

The eye / circles, and seeks
by Kenneth Irby

The eye
circles, and seeks
in the long map of California
a rest
along the Central Valley
looks down
keeping the corners out
open toward New Mexico
and the High Plains North, old
watersheds East and back again
of the spirit journey
looking for home
from the memory, and the ease
the feedback past
anything as easy as remembering
from the Marysville Buttes a cut
Northeast, up lava flows
toward Paradise, that city
and the single one
of all our meeting

to dwell *in* the flesh
a perch on one tree root
above the one stream
everflowing
that it may be the balance
exactly here where
I squat above Butte Creek

*

Streams, it must be
Strawberry Creek is one of the Rivers
of Paradise, and its canyon
the Vale of Surprise

                    and Butte Creek, far North

where I came down to earth again
painfully lacking Ishi

and uncertain of the nature color, *ch'ing* 青
 and nonetheless encountered
the firmness of *lines*
a sweat lodge on the bank
a pile of stones
and a rick of wood to stoke

I came down from the sky
or equally nowhere inside
and went underground
in order to enter the *wet,* a kinsman
that was mine from the beginning
if I had known it, I would have learned to breathe
before now, down close to the ground
as I can get

*

Of the Rivers of Paradise
three are on this earth
I have been brought to, I have been shown
which is not the same as known
any other way

California is a dry clime much of the year
and around the courses of the heart we twine
a loving mesh for those waters
we ride upon
Such a place we *learn*
The burden of knowing is *shared*
Only another can bring us to the place we yearn for
to bear
and what ease you have, you bring along with you
but even that I had to be taught

Three creeks, three friends
as close to me as those three cracks
are to the other world
of certainty

Strawberry Creek   from Lalo
Butte Creek   from Mt Goat
Nanette   from Shao

This is not Portolá's men, nor Drake's, nor even Ishi now

but crises of the common speech

*

On these verges of Cascadia
of the continent of affections
at any minute out the window

*

The chance passage of a car along Shattuck
bringing Schumann's "Träumerei"
from childhood almost palpable
this loneliness
I thought of you Lowell
going home alone
knowing you are there beyond whatever distance
Out of the light off the woodwork I see your figure
I want it to get up and walk away
come back sometimes, still call
this same house home

Enough to carry a perch of me
on the ridges of this vast landscape
this shape of California in the single closed eye
fully as far as you are, a touch
there in the hot imperial graben of salt and dates
since there is no holding the expanse of speech
except along a line of blood
between us

*

Looking down into the stream to see what passes through me

the sun at the steps of the butte
triangulates cuts of the barranca
as I squat here —
        I am made *air's*   eye
by birth, and breath
and journey of the spirit
above the earth —
        I am made *earth's*   belly

crawling back inside on my hands and knees
naked in the dark
mud up my asshole —
           fires's   cock
off heated stones
and steam, to lead back sweat —
                     water's   tongue
jumping in the creek, freezing my balls tight
 where the sun is brightest

looking inward at the home cosmography of the flow

*

The fog comes back again, cooling
across the air the islands of the heart
Fall comes back, I want to start again
on a long journey across the land
an urgency
to outdistance the fall of leaves
or on this coast, into the approaching winter rains
find the season of regeneration
crossing and recrossing the ridges of the Coast Range
seeking Cascadia

beyond the fall of anything but continents
or the rise of any but the Great Seasons
of the Great Year, this the Autumn
into the Solstice, and the Water Bearer to come

*

My head rolls on the rim of the world
My eyes are not what I see with
In the basket, in the valley
In the creek bed under the water

Lowell's Dream
by Will Staple

You and I were standing outside
    this building at the University
vibrant excited women
were asking our advice
    on how they could feel
        more complete within themselves
we toned each response
directly to the person on whose palm
    we gazed
we could pick from all of the women
    the one
who could answer that question
    for us
how could we make each other more complete?

Sierra Buttes '87
by Will Staple

Preaching simplicity
"All you need is the flesh on your bones
and an attention to the day's unfolding
revelation"

Pine needles shimmered in the tops of trees
sunbeams pierce the branches
We breathe deep, climbing steepens

"A forgiving gratitude
with a quivering
delicate edge"
is what I'd call it

Lowell also claimed
"Exertion is pleasure"

I assured him I would quote him
somewhere further up the trail.

Polar Bear Head #1
by Will Staple

Rita
was Lowell's girl
in the smallest
    house in Nevada City.

It was so small
she cut off the
    head
so she could put her rug down.

I got the head
and fitted its teeth
    around the front luggage rack bar
    on top of my old VW bug
I drove it like that
    for a year

the eyes staring
straight ahead
down the road.

Nov 17 Sutra
nanao speaking to lowell & me
by Will Staple

in desert cave, so light, so strong.   far
from moving graveyard — vast ghost town
visited by millions of weekend tourists
                one last time.

Had i the chance; priests
for calm end of survival; faint
when realizing how far is left to walk.

motionless in trance, open-eyed coma,
    no consciousness.   my spirit listening,
leaves me   vacant   to soar   so far —

goodby people civilization roles actors,
goodby future goodby life, there is no life.
only;   Bright silence of the sun.

      Fasting;
completely stop outside...try for yourself,
from inside; then you see whole world
(not small part the "agents" display
"we are content cause it doesn't seem worthwhile
to get ahead of anybody"
so suffer the same   limitations as they.)

to cut off all desire; that is biggest desire
      ("possible to disenchant yourself
        by indulgence to grow more tired?")

need so strong inner demand
    you can't have desire.
        cleaning,
cleansing power, desire comes up at first
but such a power   changing to cleansing power —
you become desire itself
then you forget desire, you are nothing.

no life, no future , no like or dislike,
no individuality;
if you have desire
            you have individuality
but if you have no more desire
            you are no more individual.

God is silence, keeps always silence
mt. stream bubbling – carrying down to ocean,
emptiness to emptiness, giving more – easily,
            learning to give more easy.

Editors' Note: This poem and the next one (Bristlecone Pine) were previously published in
Coyote Run: Poems by Will Staple, Gene Anderson, Lowell Levant

Bristlecone Pine
by Will Staple

sagebrush pale green
wind skinned legs on bare shale
ground strewn with power sticks
we feel no need to touch.

trees emerge around each bend on northslopes.
being not so numerous
each can be all the more prized.

cones on green branches spring
from seemingly lifeless trucks
worn smoothy with sharp edges
by sand sleet rain and snow
          relentless.

                       ***

a smooth tongue shows a skilled liar,
but a good way to bluff;
pretend you're thinking it just then;
   "i can see it now
    as if before my very eyes"
hand motions and smiling gestures
   can fill the hesitations.

she's in the position to light down wind.
we can't pass it out of the hollow tree
to him who found this place, who just
pushed a stick inside which broke.
Stuck pipe! retired at a sacred site,
severance pay spent in a whiff
of half a dozen illuminating passes.
gone into the realm of relics, she leans on
my other arm asleep near the hand exposed
to the increasing wind. Shadows deepen,
eye lashes flicker in near motionless bodies
warmed by a special touch, each's warmth
caught in the other.
the many slender trucks   of the bristlecone tremble.

small needled clusters sway on barked branches,
sharp knives and deamon forks flash   into
High Altitude, which is also behind   and below us.

wind dies down considerably.

only other pipe the scary one
"my personal shaman do you approve?"
"not for me, here's the matches"
i hesitate to inflict me on you.
i'd hate to start singing
"i wish i could write it down"
at the top of my lungs.

chill, cold, want to get out of it.
uphill clear and rocky, the way to
the vision tops blocked with snow
an omen not for us to now go.

we walk down above the far below
stretch out each a different way
                over the rise.
Cacot i pass on peeing, his name giver
died this year but was very old
                and had told a lot.
Raphael was much more sudden;
"the police who took him from
williams to flagstaff hospital say
cirrhosis of the liver
but he walked out the canyon
no long before
        just like you or me."
four sips above the old snow, water felt
like hernitos green without the sting,
more power to let the energy to face
all feelings and failing, clingings
and rapture   inconsolable, irrevocable
irretrievable, flow, each instant
            into the next.
                        ***

under edge of tree cut sky, to them
the sing must be tasted like a wind;
Time has washed clean all frailty;
only the true survives, the essential core,
all else...   washed clean, blown away.

       bare bristlecone
    points the way
    the earth ascends thru space

silence or so long, underneath instinctual
silence of so long, underneath, intuitive
it is the earth our body cuts
the sun lit sky with, in the shadow
in the shade resting too long
      we don't do anyone any good
          we're not in jail.

hilltop, different from a canyon
bristlecone, different from cottonwood
connected without trail
grafted to the same memory
visionary run, where you can have all
you're ever wanted the way you always
wanted it, as much as you rapture-filled

want, delight in, desire, or
you can take the path that no one has ever trod
or ever will again, alone or with a diminishing band,
sing the oldest songs, those never sung
or cease being sung, somewhere deep
within the heart of this oldest tree.
                    ***

as the sun set chilly
thru four needle clusters
    we hang over looking down
on sierra snow shadow'd range
      go for the car
      while light remains.

A Trucker Named Lowell
By Will Staple

you work so hard up in the cab
making the connections
        that keep the world working and running
the back alleys wide enough
        the short cut way thru smooth easy
no bounce around
    shift struggle
above the curved highway danger
        but for a twitch of finger
            that makes it all all right
holding life in one hand
        instead of the first beer of the day
and the wheel
        the sweet turning wheel
            in the other.

TO LOWELL LEVANT
by Doug Palmer

We will go beckoning
                    always
            won't we
                we will go

    And there
            we will rise our eyes
                        up to see

                leaves on
        many trees
                    many leaves

                    And our eyes first
        then fingers
                and before
                    thinking it out

                    we will

                move beckoning
            with
        the leaves   the trees

Editors' Note: This was previously published in <u>*Poems Read in the Spirit of Peace and Gladness*</u>

(untitled)

for Lowell
        after before.
            each time
                flown
            like a good
                big bird
        the full-bosomed
                & joyous
            stance, you
                are

                Doug Palmer 1967

Desert in Fall
by Gene Anderson

Desert fall: streams dry
to boulder-fields. Brush turns gray.
Tumbleweeds blow
on violent north wind.

Seeds drop like rain
from goosefoot and wild tarragon.
Saltbush sheds white scales
on bare sand.

The desert flowers
withered long ago.
A few pale tan stalks
line long-dry channels.

The one flower returns
on the night wind
that howls round my poor house.
Alone as always

I dream of sun
On long-closed roads.
The tracks washed out. The mountain
closed on its unknown graves.

Nocturne
by Gene Anderson

Alone with two dogs
I watch Orion
rise in diamond light
over Paivika's black hill.

His star-dogs follow him,
huge and pure white
on this night of wind
beyond the worlds.

Thin cloud
Disperses beyond Paivika mountain.
The rivers of air
Fall still. No twig moves.

Dear ones,
friends, loves, black dog, yellow dog,
I wait for you
with music or silence,

your bodies transformed
into holy light,
into endless star paths
that rise without setting.

What's left of you
by Caren Levant

Polished hand-picked rocks
    once sentry to all your special places
        lost now to time
            never to return home
Dust covered books
    filled with fingered pages
        yellowed and musty from the want of years
            (nature, poetry, literature)
Journals
    once a promising place
        to bury your wailings
            and wantings,
        now waiting for release,
            ink quietly fading in retreat
                as the pages yellow and curl from the heavy cigar laden air
Your treasures
    a safe driver pin
    a 15 year coin
    some driftwood from ?
Boxes and boxes and boxes of life
    towering above
    never unpacked
        now headed for the junkyard
for lack of a need to know
    or a want to know
Things become mountains of years
    filed and piled
        and then hidden away
            in corners and cupboards and teapots and closets.
Drawers and drawers and drawers
    of papers and scraps
        meaning something once
            now a big mystery
                a puzzle without a key
symbols of you
      your life in space
      your place in time
        your imprint on the universe
          lost forever
                to dust

Your Addiction
by Caren Levant

Your addiction
    became my addiction
        his addiction now
We are all addicts in the world of enchantments
    unable to deny the instantaneous pleasures
      that call our name
Impulsively jumping
    from one high to another
      resting on downers to
          balance the flow
escaping the boredom
    and slowness of time
      inching forward by seconds
    each minute the same as the next,
      the last
Alternate visions replacing the real
    the dreams no longer static and
      expected,
the daytime
    an endless barrage of unanswered questions
      the answers so simple
      when clouded in Ecstasy
      the happiness
      instant and consistent
    the blue pill
      the red one,
      the powder
        the junk
      swallow or sniff
      inhale or inject
death takes you slowly
and you have no time
to repent.

2010

For Lowell
by Caren Levant

Your breath is the wind
  on my cheeks in Muir Woods
The wind thru my hair
     whipping through trees
    that beckon
        that stand mighty
Tall trees
     that look down on me
        after years of stretching upwards
          into the clouds

You sat by this tree
  in a different time,
    ran your fingers
      across its bark
      and
        howled
          at the moon

I climbed as high
     as the branches would take me

but I couldn't find you

anywhere

2010